WHO
DO YOU SAY
THAT I AM?

WHO DO YOU SAY THAT I AM?

The Christian Understanding of Christ and Antisemitism

Joseph E. Monti

PAULIST PRESS
New York/Ramsey

Library of Congress
Catalog Card Number: 83-82023

ISBN: 0-8091-2598-6

Published by Paulist Press
545 Island Road, Ramsey, N.J. 07446

Printed and bound in the
United States of America

CONTENTS

PREFACE

The majority of this essay was prepared for delivery in the spring of 1982 at the Huntsville-Vanderbilt Study Forum in Huntsville, Alabama. Professor and Rabbi Peter Haas of Vanderbilt University and I shared a lecture series entitled *Church and Synagogue: Building the Basis for Dialogue.* The Introduction and the first three chapters were prepared specifically for the forum. Notes for the fourth chapter were presented in a dialogue with Professor Haas. The Appendix was prepared specifically for this publication and is based on a prior effort to introduce beginning seminarians to the fundamentals of critical and constructive Christian theology.

I am most appreciative to Frank Broyles, executive director of the Huntsville-Vanderbilt Study Forum, for his invitation to present these lectures and to the participants who continue to demonstrate the interest in community-based theological education as well as its ecumenical viability. Thanks are also due to the editors of Paulist Press for their positive consideration of my work and to my wife, Davelyn Vignaud Monti, for her editorial assistance and her constant call for clear expression and succinct style.

INTRODUCTION

THE CHALLENGE OF DIALOGUE

Real dialogue is always a challenging undertaking. And when the partners have a heritage of suspicion, antipathy, and even persecution, the prospects of success seem overwhelmingly poor. Christians and Jews are obviously of the same religious family. However, it is not uncommon that what starts as a family quarrel often escalates to tragic proportions. This essay is offered as a contribution toward establishing basic foundations for a renewal of religious and theological dialogue between Christianity and Judaism, Christians and Jews. I write self-consciously as a Christian ethicist and theologian. I write first for Christians who are struggling with the implications for their own faith and tradition when they are called upon to give complete religious and theological affirmation of Judaism. Such an affirmation does not suggest that there be total agreement between Christians and Jews, much less a reunion between Church and Synagogue. Rather, as a foundation for real dialogue, Christians and Jews alike are called to affirm an initial validity of their respective ways of faith—ways of faith that exhibit certain similarities as well as basic differences. Thus, Jews, who for good historical reasons have felt compelled to withhold basic judgments of validity for Christianity, may be interested in still another effort to discuss the necessary conditions for mutual affirmation. I consider such mutual affirmation a religious, theological, and moral imperative of any tradition that maintains an understanding of common humanity rooted in faith in a Creator God.

3

SETTING THE STAGE FOR DIALOGUE

In the beginning of the Christian-Jewish quarrel, the demography noted a Jewish majority and a Christian minority. The New Testament era was a time of building a self-identity for this Christian minority. Christian confession and theology developed in such a way that it soon became impossible to keep any sort of dual identity of Christian-Jew or Jewish-Christian. By the time of the New Testament texts, it simply was no longer possible to reconcile the main traditions of Judaism with the new Christian confession.

After initial periods of conflict with the parent body of Judaism and with the dominant Roman culture and society, Christianity began to exercise an important influence. Christianity was a religion that in principle did not highlight ethnic identity or emphasize a territorial home—one that could in principle become universal. It attracted many sincere and real converts to its new confession as well as those who saw in Christianity a new ideology that could be used for social and political purposes. The conversion of the Roman emperor Constantine at the begining of the fourth century epitomized this latter interest.[1] Therefore, because of both its own inherent religious appeal as well as its utility as a force for social and political unification, in three hundred years Christianity became the dominant religion of the "civilized" Western world.

With Christianity's emergence as a majority, the most intense and tragic conflicts with its parent Judaism took shape. As Christianity struggled for self-identity, Judaism went into a new *diaspora*—spreading itself again far from its religious and ethnic home. Even before the achievement of the Christian majority, Judaism was no longer a national religion or temple cult. Judaism would remain what was essentially a sub-culture, never to regain ascendancy until the modern era. As the majority in the Jewish-Christian family, the mainstream of Christianity became less and less tolerant of its ancient parent and now-elder sibling. The New Testament and the writings of the Greek and Roman "Fathers" contain scores of anti-Jewish phrases and polemics.[2] In the earliest days of the Christian minority—the days when Christianity lacked any real socio-political power—such writings could be understood as marking the intensity of a religious family quarrel and the search for a new self-identity by a fledgling religion. However, with its own rise to ascendancy and its new liaisons with the state, Christianity's now dominant interests in theological and socio-political conformity led to intolerant and persecutive practices.

The history of Christian-Jewish relations is clear. The conclusion that Christians have been the offending party and Jews the offended is unavoidable. Contemporary discussions and documentations of the Christian offense and Jewish response abound in both their historical occurrence and development.[3] It is only appropriate, fair, and just that those who have been most offended describe their own experience of oppression and persecution. Therefore, the appropriate opening for any actual dialogue between Christians and Jews—Church and Synagogue—is for Jews to define and describe what they have endured historically at the hands of the Christian majority. It is for them to frankly and understandably confess their own suspicion and hesitation when cast into a majority Christian culture and society.[4]

The responsibility of Christians is first to listen, to learn and be reminded, to overcome initial defensive reactions. Only after such respectful, attentive, and even sorrow-filled listening can Christians begin to actively respond and the dialogue take shape. The challenge of Christian response to anti-Jewish and indeed anti-Semitic thought and action can and should take a variety of forms. As historical experience indicates, one might distinguish anti-Judaism (religious prejudice) from anti-Semitism (racial prejudice). However, as history also indicates, the two often have not been separated, with the former setting the stage for the more deadly latter. Guilt, shame, conversion, and transformation are all appropriate responses to this tragic part of Christian-Jewish history. Yet as difficult as such responses may seem to some, *they are finally not enough.* What is required of Christians in a situation of real dialogue with Jews is a re-examination of our basic heritage of self-identity and self-understanding. *What has emerged as a moral challenge of the gravest proportions for Christians must now become a confessional and theological challenge.* What we confess to believe and how we explain those beliefs in theological ways can no longer (if indeed this has ever been the case) withstand the inevitable moral challenge of practical experience. No matter what the intention of our basic confessions and theologies, no matter how they may have been misused, we must finally face the question of their practical moral effects in history. In short, *the Christian legacy of anti-Judiasm and anti-Semitism challenges Christian faith and theology at its very core—our own confession and explanation of Jesus as the Christ.*[5] Certainly Christian faith and theology have contributed much to the human search for meaning, our common quests for truth and right. But we must admit that our Christologies—at least in their effects—have had a dark side as well.[6] And while it may be true that Christian faith and theology do not *logically* lead to the persecution of Jews, they have been used historically to "justify" such persecution. Furthermore, it is hard to deny that much, if not most, of our Christological tradition has both *logically and historically* led to certain anti-Jewish religious prejudice, if only of a tolerant liberal variety—on the one hand, maintaining the right of Judaism's existence and free practice, and on the other, seeing it as finally misguided.

The four chapters of this book intend to draw interested Christians into a discussion of the foundations for an adequate theological and moral response to our own legacy of anti-Judaism and anti-Semitism. We will try to move beyond the shock of initial shame and guilt to a re-examination of our own self-identity and self-understanding. In short, we will concentrate on the core of Christian faith and theology. This defining center of Christianity is captured in the New Testament story where Jesus addresses Peter with the question: "Who do you say that I am?" Peter's answer succinctly states the basic Christian faith and presents the key terms for any future Christological inquiry: "You are the Christ, the Son of the living God."[7] To remain vital and morally self-critical, our own religious self-identity and theological self-understanding demand that we hear again Jesus' question, faithfully join in Peter's confession, and finally take up the inevitable, continuing task of interpreting its theological meaning in our own time.

OUTLINE OF CHAPTERS

The four chapters of this essay are focused toward the moral challenge of building the basis for an adequate Christian response in any proposed dialogue with Jews. Chapter I, "Interrelating Faith and Theology: The Status of Christian Claims," is in general an exercise in fundamental theology. We will inquire into the phenomenon of religious and theistic faith in general, attempt to understand the nature of constructive theological discourse and the implications of its inter-relationship with faith confessions, and set our tradition of multiple Christological formulations and explanations in this foundational context. This chapter intends to discover the proper status of religious and theological claims (the nature of their truth) in general, and of Christian claims in particular, especially for Christian Christological claims with respect to Judaism. In an Appendix to the total essay I will address the status of the maximal statement of the Christian claim under the title "I am *the* way, *the* truth and *the* life."

Chapter II, "Christological Origins," is an exercise in historical and biblical theology. It presents a summary, general profile and overview of New Testament Christological faith—the foundational background, substantive confession, and initial theological presentations of the Church's earliest struggles with its own self-identity and self-understanding. The chapter ends with a basic statement of the Christological paradox of the New Testament witness—the paradoxical inter-relationship of divinity and humanity which would become a theological problem for the next generations.

Chapter III, "Paradox and Problem" is an exercise in systematic theology with attention to historical origins of Christological doctrine and dogma, along with further notes for the process of Christological reconstruction. This chapter addresses the attempt of theology to create meaningful models for the Christologial paradox as an activity of theological imagination. It examines the movement of the definition of Christology from paradox to problem in the Councils of Nicea and Chalcedon with attention to the functional strengths, weaknesses and dangers of the resulting orthodoxy of doctrine and dogma. The chapter concludes with the notes for Christological reinterpretation and reconstruction, as well as a brief note on basic contemporary trends.

Chapter IV, "Notes for a Reconstructed Christology," takes up the constructive challenge of presenting a Christology that is both faithful for Christianity and non-negating for Judaism. The chapter addresses the norms for adequacy of reconstructed Christologies (norms of truth, of right and good, and of fidelity). It then presents basic theological notes that summarize the concepts and terms which are to make up an adequate Christology; it reviews the traditional phrases and paradigms for such theological modeling, and, finally, it suggests how these concepts, terms, and models ought to be reconstructed in a single suggestion for a faithful, non-negating Christological paradigm—a paradigm that both affirms Christian faith and at the same time allows for the affirmation of Jewish faith in a *normative Christological metaphor and model of dialogic communication.*

Finally, all of the chapters in this essay are presented with the conviction that there will remain significant differences in Christian and Jewish confessions and theologies. At the same time, I am convinced that Christianity—in its faith and theology—*does not need to negate Judaism* to be faithful, *nor can* it if it is to be moral.

Chapter I

INTERRELATING FAITH
AND THEOLOGY:
THE STATUS OF
CHRISTIAN CLAIMS

INTRODUCTION:
THE BASIC CHRISTIAN QUESTION

The basic question of the Christian religion is framed for us in the New Testament story where Jesus asks his disciples "Who do you say that I am?" This question implies several important understandings. First, *the issue is not self-evident,* but rather controversial—many answers could be put forth. Many answers were put forth in Jesus' day and in every epoch thereafter, including our own. Second, *the issue calls for a personal engagement of interpretation and decision*—a commitment rooted in intense personal and interpersonal experience. Third, *the question demands an answer.* And on that answer Christianity, as the comprehensive interpretation of human experience, will be accepted or rejected.

THE IMPLICATIONS OF
CHRISTIANITY'S QUESTION

Christianity's question implies even more basic "truths" of this religion and of religion in general. First, we should understand that all religious truth emerges in plural forms that change and develop throughout the ebb and flow of history. Truth itself is always situated in multi-faceted and shifting contexts. *Truth is in motion.*

At the same time that it is *plural*, all religious truth—and truth itself—is *unique*. At this level of universal religious meaning—this comprehensive level of interpreting the meaning of human life itself—truth is more of an *engaged experience* unique to persons and groups than the result of logical deduction or simple physical demonstration. In short, religious truth is grounded in experiences of faith.

Therefore, when we come to the basic Christian question ("Who do you say that I am?"), we know that we are first at a level of language and knowledge that is religious rather than scientific, that is more mysterious than crystal clear. Because religious and faith experiences are both *unique* (special to the person and group) and *plural* (the special experiences of many people and groups), all constructive[1] answers to religious questions will be personally plural as well. No single rational explanation or doctrinal formulation can exhaust the richness of meaning of what some experience as a statisfactory interpretation of their lives in the world. All constructive attempts at rational theological explanations of faith experiences must function as second-level discourse—starting from and returning to the primary level of engaged personal and interpersonal experience.

Consequently, the question—"Who do you say that I am?"—can be adequately addressed only when we come to understand it first as a religious question, one that calls forth faith commitments. Only then can it be engaged in a constructive theological way. From this theological perspective, the question has called forth a plurality of historically conditioned answers, asked again and again in each succeeding generation of Christian life—a continuing quest that has challenged Christianity to maintain itself as a tradition and heritage of human meaning and moral action in the world.

THE FOUNDATION OF
THE CHRISTIAN CONFESSION:
THE ONE AND THE MANY

Now that the basic question is set, our proper pluralistic and historically condition context laid out, can there be any real content for an answer? Have I stressed the norms of pluralism and historical relativity to such a degree that we are left with the conclusion that any answer will do as long as it is sincere? Is there no common foundation upon which to build and, indeed, to critique the multitude of answers of each generation of Christian believers?

Again, we must return to the scriptural story. Jesus' question stimulated Peter's reply: "You are the Christ, the Son of the living God." This was Peter's confession of faith that stands as the basic foundation of all future Christian confessions and Christological explanations. Whatever pluralities of confessional statements or of philosophical or theological explanations have been and are now being entertained by Christians, the basic terms and implications of Peter's straightforward confession must now be treated as normative. This single and foundational confession of faith grounds all Christological reflections in their attempt to give some coherent and cognitive theological content—some sensible explanation—to and for this faith experience.

Even though Christian confessions and Christological explanations will remain plural, Peter's confession stands as the one ground of that plurality. All other confessional statements and theological formulations stand as qualifications of this one. "You," *the man Jesus,* "are the Christ," *the one chosen, the anointed one of Yahweh, the Messiah.* As the Christ-Messiah, you are "the Son of the living God"—*God's emissary of salvation, the presence of God among us, the mediator of our presence to God who remains with us despite all evidence to the contrary.*

FAITH AND THEOLOGY

We have now come to a point of contact between faith and theology—contact between the unique experience of faith commitment and the demand to give some coherence and order to that experience, the demand for rational explanation. This contact between faith and theology is inevitable, yet it requires great care in its analysis. On the one hand, we are called to keep the sense of the interpersonal uniqueness of faith alive—the sense of responsive confession. On the other, we are challenged by our common need for rational explanation to give some ordered and systematic account of our confession—to explain our faith as it were, to talk about it in rational ways, and even to watch over it critically and guard it lest it lead us astray and do damage to others.

Again, it is important to keep in mind that religious truth is focused primarily at experiential levels of faith and commitment—at the confessional level of primary religious discourse. As I have argued, faith confessions by their nature are both unique and plural—*unique* to personal and interpersonal experiences of meaning, understanding, and commitment; *plural* insofar as such experiences cannot be logically required and proven or singularly demonstrated. At this level we confess, witness, proclaim and celebrate our faith as a self and group expression, and for the consideration and edification of others. In the case of all religious traditions, however, and certainly for Christians, basic foundational faith confessions can and do become normative—the one foundation that grounds all plurality of expression.[2]

At the point of interpersonal, intersocietal, and transcultural sharing and communication—at the point where those who have shared primary and foundational religious experiences want to share with others—the *second level* of religious discourse emerges. Here, *theological discourse* begins to exercise its cognitive rational interests. Theology is by nature a *theoretic mode* of human speech—a systematic attempt to explain primary faith confessions in predominantly philosophical ways.

This faith that emerges from experiences of existential and interpersonal engagement is in fact an experience of *acceptance* and "letting go": the acceptance of a *supra*-rational interpersonal encounter that in its depth transcends the ordinary meaning of functional everyday existence, the "letting go" of our common notions of scientific objectivity as the only way to truth and certainty. The great paradox of our scientific culture is that as much as we long for increasing objectivity, proof, and security in our lives, in our quieter moments we know that greater truth and certainty are found at trans-scientific levels of deep personal and interpersonal experiences. In this sense the truth and certainty that come with faith are quite similar to true and certain experiences of love. Both are "falling in" experiences. We "fall into" deep and mature faith in much the same way that we "fall into" real love. Still, it is also part of our human experience that there are less mature and less personal engagements of both faith and love. We often, maybe most often, "believe" and "love" because it is the thing to do—an expectation of our socialization or the result of our processes of acculturation.

Theology, as a constructive-theoretic form of discourse, intends to give some explanation for our faith in a logical, coherent fashion. Theology tries to answer the questions of why we have fallen into faith in this or that particular way, and the meaning and implications of that faith. In one sense such theological theorizing seems inappropriate and even impossible—like trying to rationally explain why we have fallen in love with this or that person, and gauging the implications of that love for the course of our life. Theology is thus limited and always somewhat unsatisfactory. On the other hand, if our faith (as does all mature faith) involves an interest in proclaiming the "good news" that we have found and sharing it with others, then we can expect rational inquiries to ensue. We are challenged by our own and others' interests in coherence and order to offer some sort of explanation. At the same time, theological discourse presents us with the opportunity to measure the implications and effects of our most intense "faith-feelings" in the world.

In one sense faith experiences and religious feelings are always true insofar as they are sincere. In another, such feelings of the "heart" cannot in themselves critically guide their own effects in the world. The truth of sincere feeling and undeniable experience is not enough for the truth of cogent and rational explanation or moral action. The contact between faith and theology mirrors the common tension that we all experience between our affairs of the "heart" and those of the "head"—feeling and thinking, emotion and reason. Feeling without reason is indiscriminate, undirected, and uncritical. However, reason without feeling is lifeless, dispassionate, and sterile. Therefore, we can say that faith without theology is blind; theology without faith is dead.[3]

Although I have distinguished faith and theology in a temporal and logical way, they are in fact never separated in any religious phenomenon. Religious experiences will finally demand some sort of initial identification and articulation—a basic confession that makes use of fundamental theological concepts and phrases.[4] Theology, when pursued from within the confines of participation in religious experience will always be grounded upon and influenced by faith. I have called this type of theology "constructive" because it reflects from the milieu of faith, gathers its sense and meaning initially from faith commitments, and has as its general intent the enhancement of those commitments. In gauging the status of Christian claims for Jesus, it is important to keep this constructive principle in mind: *the sense and persuasive character of Christological claims and explanations can attain the full status of truth only for those who have first "fallen into" the faith in some way.*

Certainly, it is possible to pursue an interest and expertise in theology in a non-constructive and analytic way—to study theology from an historical, cultural, socio-political, or generally academic interest. This, however, is *not* our task or interest. In a dialogue with Jews we want to be *full partners* rather than only dispassionate and analytic observers. We have inherited the faith and theologies of those who have gone before us. Indeed, we can be ennobled by their accomplishments just as we must be saddened and ashamed of their crass failures—especially of our traditional and inherited Christian failure to affirm Judaism and respect Jews. To respond adequately to this dark side of our Christian tradition, we must become full partners in dialogue with Jews. We must speak as believers and reflect theologically from the perspective of that deep commitment. Any attempt on our part to dilute our core faith confession or falsely accommodate our tradition of Christological claims to advance the dialogue would be a dual infidelity—an infidelity to our own self-defining faith and an infidelity to our Jewish partners who should expect integrity and honesty, no matter how initially disagreeable, as first norms for successful dialogue.

With this basic foundation being established, the remainder of my essay will concentrate primarily upon the second-level discourse of theological language and reflection. All the while, however, the basic confession and practice of Christian faith in the world will be in the background as a "bankboard," so to speak, for judging the adequacy of our theological interpretations and speculations. The basic existential integrity of Christianity is established in its foundation by its confession of faith in Jesus the Christ, the "Son of the living God." All constructive theological theorizing must finally be judged on how it relates to this basic Christian confession—how our theology is *faithful* to the faith, how it *enhances* understanding and practice of the faith, and how it *reconstructs* the faith to be a more critical and vital promotion of the true, the right, and the good in any given historical era.

I have argued that even though faith is the foundation of the constructive theological enterprise, faith itself *needs* theological interpretation and explanation. To be a people with others in the world, to share the world in a human, humane and, indeed, Christian way, the Church must not only be a community of faith but a community of theological discourse as well—discourse that gives critical reasons and coherent, relatively satisfactory explanations for its own beliefs and practices. Again, as I have argued, such theological activity gives the Church an opportunity to check its beliefs and practices not only for sincerity and fidelity, but also for its pragmatic truth and morality—the truthfulness of its effects in the world and its promotion of the morally right and good. *Truth and morality go hand-in-hand.* To be true, our faith must be honest and sincere—the experiences about which we speak must have in fact happened to us in some way, functioning as comprehensive interpretations of the meaning of our human existence. At the same time the validation of our claims for truth in faith must also be rooted in theological articulations and moral practices that promote frameworks of meaning and explanation which influence and promote a just, peaceful, and loving world, all within the context of changing cultures and societies.

Just as faith confessions among the world religions are unique to multiple and interpersonal experience and to particular forms of speech and self-expression, theologies are varied and changeable because of the variable canons of rationality and explanation. In other words, theologies vary and change because philosophies, sociologies, psychologies and the other human sciences utilized by theology are multiple, developing and regressing in the flow of historical movement. However, amid this plurality and change all religions—Christianity included—can be put to critical-pragmatic tests. Basic questions that interrelate truth and morality can be asked: What in fact do particular faith confessions effect in the world? What do they promote? How are we transformed by them? What do they proclaim for the human future? What do they project as our liberating human destiny? How do they deal with the limits of fated circumstances? No matter how sincere our faith confessions, they must finally be put to critical-pragmatic tests if they are to *remain* in their own truth as proclamations and promotions of the right and the good for humankind.

THE FOUNDATIONAL CHRISTIAN ERA: CONFLICT, DEBATE, AND DECISION

Interrelating Faith and Theology

The challenge of all social religious experience is to engage in a mutual interchange between faith and theology. The first followers of Jesus took up this challenge in their attempt to answer the question: "Who do you say that I am?" From the original plurality of confessions and primary theological articulations, Peter's answer gained ascendancy and became paradigmatic—"You are the Christ, the Son of the living God." With this confession and the incipient theological explanation (found first in the writings of Paul and then throughout the New Testament), the break with Judaism was complete. What traditional Jews could not say about Jesus was now being said by Christians—those who in fact became Christians in this basic confession.

Now the challenge would be to transmit and share this confession for ages to come, explaining the meaning and the interrelationship of its terms and concepts. How is this man of the world, Jesus, associated with God, our Creator and Sustainer? What is new about the salvation both accomplished and promised in Jesus the Christ? What effect will this faith have on our lives in the world? How are we to relate to each other and to those of our own religious family who have heard but have not and cannot "fall into" faith in this way—our Jewish sisters and brothers?

The Theological Foundations of the Christian-Jewish Conflict

If we keep in mind the conditions for the emergence of religious faith and its relation to theological explanation, we can see that it was not the Christian confession of faith as such that caused so much repression and tragic persecution of Jews; rather, it was the understanding and, indeed, *the misunderstanding of the status of Christian claims and theological explanations* that did the damage. Moreover, as an ecclesiology developed that eventually began to see Church and state in a concert that demanded socio-political as well as theological conformity, the problems of Christian-Jewish relations quickly compounded.

Therefore, it was this unique combination of the misunderstanding of the status of Christian religious and theological claims, along with the Church's historical development of intimate relations with the state, that led to our own tragic history with Judaism. Over the centuries the Christian Church has for the most part learned—often grudgingly—an historical lesson about being too closely involved with the state. (I say "for the most part" because we are witnessing in our own time and culture movements that repeat this classical mistake. It is certainly true that historical lessons must be continually relearned.)[5] However, the mistaken understanding of the status of religious and theological claims, for the Christian Church and for religions in general, still needs correction. The metaphor of youthful rebellion and revolution gives us some rationale for this mistake in foundational Christianity. But such a metaphor has long since lost its applicability; the same rationale no longer applies for us.

If we keep in mind the analogy between faith and love, we can see that we ought to have no real problems with accepting a plurality of intensely personal experiences of "true faith" or "true love" to exist side by side in the world. As a rule, we have no real interest or desire to negatively criticize or persecute those who fall in love in different ways with different people (though we *still* do so at times if the difference in love is too great). In like manner, can we not say that a Christian has fallen into faith in one way, a Jew in another? Can we not say that both are sincere and truthful, and that at least for the time being (before the necessary critical-pragmatic tests), both are true and therefore acceptable?

At the level of rational theological discourse, however, we often face what we think are unsolvable logical difficulties. How can there be a plurality of rational truths? If *this* is true then its *contrary* must be false. If Jesus in some objective or quasi-objective way is *the* way, *the* truth, and *the* life because he has both said and demonstrated it, then he is this for all. The worst that we can say about those who do not accept Jesus as the Christ is that they are evil; the best that we can say is that they are blind or misguided. In either case, they are wrong.

I would call both of these negative judgments forms of religious and theological prejudice based on a lack of understanding of the nature of theological discourse and its relation to faith—a mistaken understanding of the status of Christian claims. Theology is not a science in the narrow sense. Faith experiences are not grounded in objective scientific demonstrations *for all to see.* Rather, as I have argued, they are grounded in phenomenal experiences—*deep experiences of interpersonal engagement and commitment*—experiences, if you will, of the heart. Mature faith events are happenings and, like love, they cannot be coerced. They are of a peculiar sort of objectivity—the objectivity of one who declares himself or herself to us[6] in a reality that cannot be denied. As phenomenal realities, faith events and love events must be plural, unique (as special), and true.

Since constructive theology emerges from and returns to this foundational faith context, its own form of rational discourse is marked by faith's characteristics. Theology is a special form of rational language. It, too, must remain plural and change in its attempts to gather sense, order, coherence, and application from faith events. Nor can theological agreement like faith adherence be personally, rationally, or morally coerced. We cannot force faith experiences nor demand theological agreement, just as we cannot *force* love or *demand* that our intended accept *our* reasons or *our* explanations for our love. Christians are confessionally and theologically in the world in one way, Jews in another. Certainly, most of our being in the world is the same. But this one thing is different: what Christians say about Jesus and how (in principle) this saying ought to transform their perspective on the world and their life in it, Jews cannot say. This does not mean that Christians and Jews do not share many of the same perspectives and ways of living. It does mean that the *proximate* subject of their faith and religious life (for Christians, Jesus Christ) is different. Be that as it may, both religions are challenged by the terrors and hopes of the same human history. We both have enough terrors and need enough hope to share at least part of the burden and responsibility of building the divine-human dwelling on earth—a dwelling that must include all of God's creation and all of God's people who, by the very fact that they are human, are chosen for goodness and life.

THE CHALLENGES AND DEMANDS
OF ADEQUATE CHRISTOLOGIES

To this point I have attempted to set a context for responding to the problem at hand—the tradition of Christian negation of Judaism and its attendant conflicts and tragedies. Our discussion thus far has led us to a point that calls for a summary outline of the conditions for adequate Christologies—those that are faithful as well as critically challenging, coherent, and right; Christologies that do not negate Judaism. The proper understanding of the nature of confessional and theological discourse and the relationship between faith and theology lead to three major challenges for adequate Christologies.

First, we are challenged to present Christologies that remain faithful and enhance the Christian confession—the foundational confession of Jesus as the Christ, "the Son of the living God." In this sense not any Christology will do, but only those that remain faithful to this informing confession that establishes Christianity as a unique and integral religion. The challenge of fidelity leads to the demand for integrity—the demand for maintaining the sense of wholeness and fullness of Christianity's claim to be a comprehensive interpretation of the meaning of human existence.

Second, we are challenged to maintain the vitality of Christological interpretations and formulations. In order to be faithful in passing on the tradition of Christian belief and practice through this generation to the next, we cannot only repeat past formulations. The challenge of reinterpreting and reconstructing theological systems so that they speak with critical relevance to the interests, needs, and concerns of our own time are demands of a vital and living faith. At the same time, the first material for these reinterpretations and reconstructions will be the same symbols, stories, and theological systems that we receive as our inheritance and tradition.

Third, adequate Christologies cannot *demand* universal adherence and acceptance—from those within our faith confession and especially from those outside it. The pluralism of constructive theology is a demand both of its faith foundation and of the historicity of all forms of human inquiry and theory—the changing conditions of rationality and human knowledge itself. At the same time, adequate Christologies which remain at the level of theory are true only in prospect until the challenge is met of critical-pragmatic tests of their effect on human life in the world.

With this in mind, we can begin to investigate the foundations of Christological inquiry. From this perspective we can then take up the challenge of contemporary interpretation and reconstruction. Our task is to search for Christologies that are faithful, meaningful, and moral—Christologies that do not negate Judaism. This task is formidable. We need to understand that answering the Christological question "Who do you say that I am?" is a continuing personal and theological challenge—a communal challenge for the Christian Church to advance justice, serve peace, promote well-being, and strive after love for all in the human family. We are called, in short, to love in a community of respectful dialogue with all members of God's family, and especially with the elder member of our own religious family. Our experience of the mystery of God's presence proclaimed for us in Jesus, the Christ, demands that we talk of God, act for and with God, on behalf of others, until we die.

Chapter II
CHRISTOLOGICAL ORIGINS

INTRODUCTION:
BASIC TERMS AND CATEGORIES

All Christological explanations revolve around three basic terms and categories, each of which is highlighted in Peter's confession of faith: "You are the Christ, the Son of the living God." All Christology begins and ends with a *theological understanding of God*—in Judeo-Christian theology, the God who is Creator and Sustainer, the God who is involved in human history and wills the salvation of humankind from its long list of self-imposed anxieties and terrors, from its own overwhelming penchant for sin. Christology is thus intrinsically bound with notions of creation, providence, and salvation.

The second term and category involves a *universal anthropological understanding of the human.* In this case, the man Jesus stands for every person in our human condition—persons who engage in both the joys and struggles of everyday existence. Christianity is by definition and nature an "earthy" religion—intimately involved in the everyday lives of human beings in the world.

Finally, there is the *Christic dimension* that establishes the basic mediating and interrelational aspect of all Christological explanation. The man Jesus becomes the Christ, the point of *mediating contact between God and the world.* He is the Christ, whose life, death, and continuing presence in the world proclaim the *saving presence of God with us.* Jesus the Christ is the "Son of the living God."

The basic *theological question*—"How is God related to the world?" (as opposed to the basic *theistic question,* "Does God exist?")—is answered in the basic Christological paradigm. God and world are interrelated—made present to each other—in Jesus, the Christ. Christologies take their starting point from this basic faith confession, attempting to give systematic order and rational development to this defining faith experience.

CHRISTOLOGICAL FOUNDATIONS

Intertestamental Period (30–50 C.E.)

During the time between the death of Jesus and the writing of the first New Testament texts, the new followers of Jesus struggled with their own self-understanding and self-identification. The classic struggle of all revolutionary movements was engaged; how to define oneself in light of one's parent body, in light of one's heritage and tradition. Now that they had confessed faith in Jesus as the Christ, how would the new group of believers relate to their own Jewish tradition? How much of that tradition should be retained? How much reinterpreted? How much cast off?

Their conflict was both internal and external. The internal conflict over self-understanding and self-identification was engaged most directly in a meeting recorded in Acts between Paul and Peter in Jerusalem. The debate was precisely over how the new believers were to define themselves in relation to their Jewish heritage. Paul's more radical understanding of Christianity, as not only the fulfillment of Judaism but its abrogation as well, in effect created a new *body* of believers who could finally no longer see themselves in the dual identity of Jewish-Christian. It was Paul's Christology that determined his understanding. His claims for Jesus were simply more than Judaism as a religion could absorb. It seems safe to say, then, that it was Paul who set the basic theological understanding of Christian belief and, in that, founded the organized Christian *Church.*

As in all efforts at new self-understanding and self-identification, external polemics were mixed with internal interpretations
of meaning. Paul's own radicalism certainly heightened the external conflict between the Jewish followers of Jesus and those Jews
who did not and, indeed, could not follow. The destruction of Jerusalem and the second temple in 70 C.E. by the Roman general
Titus led Christian apocalyptic writing to claim God's final ap-
proval of this new faith and incipient theology.[1]

I have used the model of a family struggle between parent
and adolescent—the struggle for mature self-understanding and
self-identification—as a metaphor for the Jewish Christian conflict in the first century. It is important for both Christians and
Jews to understand how the many polemical and anti-Jewish writings in the New Testament came to be. The struggles, though intense, were among members of the same religious and cultural
family. The Christian "child," struggling for an individual identity,
protested against many parental traditions. The Jewish parent under siege from many sources, not the least of which was a foreign
occupation of its ethnic and religious homeland, responded in
kind.

The conflict, however, was too great. The child would always
be influenced by parental traditions but would never again return
home. All faith confessions and theological explanations could
have perhaps been negotiated, save one: "Jesus, the Christ, the
Son of the living God." Paul led the new believers to *correctly* see
that their belief in Jesus was something *radically new.* At the
same time, Paul, understandably but *unfortunately* and even *in-
correctly,* led them to see their faith as not only new and different,
but as a polemical and, at times, angry *negation* of their parental
heritage.

In this, Christianity committed the error of youthful rebellion.
Interests in reformation, change, and even revolution led to con-
flictual denial of the worth of its Jewish parental heritage—a phenomenon that became historically repetitive in Christianity's
ongoing struggle with both external and internal pluralism. The
metaphor of parent-child soon became one of sibling conflict: as
the socially, culturally and politically stronger sibling, Christianity took the path of repression and persecution of its older but
weaker rival.

RELIGIOUS AND SOCIO-CULTURAL MILIEU

A great mixture of religious and socio-cultural forces existed in this intertestamental period that aided the Christian rejection of Judaism. During this time, Judaism was not of one cloth. A variety of emphases abounded. The apocalyptic and eschatological forces in Jewish religion, Greek neo-Platonic philosophy and the socio-political structure of Roman universalism each contributed to the development of the New Testament Christological rejection of Judaism. I will discuss the meaning of apocalyptic and eschatological language and the influence of Roman universalism in what follows. I will save the discussion of the important influence of Greek philosophy for our discussion of New Testament texts and the great Christological conflicts.

Apocalyptic Language and Thought

Apocalyptic language and thought forecast the "imminent events of the end" of any particular historical period or of history itself. Apocalyptic language indicates that the "time is at hand" for radical transformation—the time of "final revolt" and the "collapse of the old." It is the time for new cosmic reconstructions.[2]

It is not hard to understand how the new believers would recast their religious revolution in such solemn and dire terms—solemn, insofar as they would soon gain historical and cosmic ascendance; dire, insofar as their opponents, including the Jewish religion, would now come to their final end. As I have mentioned, the Roman destruction of Jerusalem and the second temple was considered a key event in this scenario of the end-time and final hour. John's Book of Revelation, written after Jerusalem's fall, is filled with mythic portents of apocalyptic destruction and renewal.

Eschatological Language and Thought

Eschatological language and thought are kin to the apocalyptic style. However, the stress on the final culmination and fulfillment of human history in God has a more primary theological emphasis. Both emphasize the transformation of the social and political structures of history, but the apocalyptic emphasis on predicting the "time and the hour" gives way in eschatological emphasis to a general hope and confidence that the "day of the Lord" will eventually come. Apocalyptic language uses an interpretation of present social and political events, transforming them into signs and portents of imminent destruction and renewal— "the time is at hand." The more intrinsic theological dynamic of eschatology emphasizes that the "logic" of faith and theological understanding leads to an unshakable confidence in God's final victory in the "eschaton"—the time of historical fulfillment in the kingdom and reign of God in the world. The more external commentary of apocalyptic on the events of the day and time is replaced with a quieter confidence in the eventual triumph of the good, the right, and the true.

The mixture of apocalyptic and eschatological forces in intertestamental Judaism influenced a similar mixture in the New Testament and led to what can be discerned as a certain duality of expectations, each having a profound influence on the faith and life of the early Christians. Was the "day of the Lord" at hand or was it to come in the distant future? If the time is at hand, what is needed is a purity of confession and of excited expectation for what is about to happen *to* history, *to* the world and *to* us. Thus, even though there is an excitement in apocalyptic thinking, there can also be a certain passivity.

On the other hand, if the "day of the Lord" is in the distant future, what is needed is faith confession along with developed theological explanations. Passivity gives way to *activity* in building the divine-human dwelling in the world—the Kingdom of God. What is needed is not only a *remnant of true believers* to herald the beginning of the new time, but a *universal Church,* peopled with believers and workers of all nations and cultures.

It was finally the ascendancy of eschatological over apocalyptic understandings which theologically undergirded the structural and socio-political development of the Christian Church, establishing its comprehensive moral interest. Even with this eschatological dominance, however, both forces remained alive in Christian faith and theology. Both proclaimed that it was Jesus the Christ who would bring history to its fulfillment. It was Christian belief that the old was passing away. *A new people had been chosen.*

Roman Universalism

The final element for this consideration of the religious and socio-cultural mix of intertestamental Judaism and Christianity was Roman universalism—the Roman norm of empire. If the ascendancy of eschatological understanding was the theological undergirding for the formation of the Christian *Church*, it was the Roman interest in a universal cross-cultural empire that finally led to the adoption of Christianity as the state religion. Both Church and empire shared interests in universal influence, although, at least in principle, for different purposes. Despite the universal themes in Judaism—its notion of being chosen as "the light to all nations," its understanding of the universal messianic reign of peace and justice—the ethnic and territorial character of the religion made it less apt to become a worldwide ideology useful for empire. In fact, Hellenized Judaism—diaspora Judaism influenced by Greek thought and culture—presented more prospects for becoming a universalizable philosophy and theology. However, Hellenized Judaism had its own internal conflicts with Palestinian Jewry, conflicts that were not minimized when its influence was felt in New Testament theology.

NEW TESTAMENT CHRISTOLOGY

The Defining Christian Intention

In summary, then, it is clear that the period between the death of Jesus and the first New Testament writings was a time of search for a new, unique identity for the followers of Jesus. I have stressed the struggle of Christianity with its parent Judaism. Other struggles went on in the Christian house itself. Paul's comments about "false gospels," recent discoveries that add to our knowledge of Christian-Gnostic literature,[3] an assumed multitude of other writings and traditions now lost, all attest to the fact that a plurality of confessions and incipient theologies existed during this period. Our present New Testament, however, attests to the victory of the Gospel's presentation of Peter's foundational confession. And the chief architect of that victory was undoubtedly Paul. It seems clear that New Testament faith and theology were influenced more by Paul's own Christological testament than by any other. Therefore, it is appropriate that we begin our brief summary of New Testament Christology with examples of Pauline Christological hymns. These and all of the New Testament Christological texts were the culminations of a period of struggle for self-understanding and self-identity: the followers of Jesus intended to discover who they were and how they had been transformed in terms of their own Jewish religious heritage. Their intention was to define themselves both confessionally and theologically. The New Testament accomplished the first task but only began the second. Theological inquiry into the meaning of the basic Christian confession would continue.

Pauline Christological Hymns

We will examine only three Pauline Christological hymns. Even from these three, however, we can discern a general profile of the most basic elements of the Christian confession of faith and the basic categories of New Testament Christology. It is not the case that each of the hymns contain every element of this profile, but taken together they offer a general and early Christological portrait. Though influenced by its own contemporary culture, this New Testament Christological portrait as a whole was a radical departure from Jewish traditions.[4]

The basic characteristics of New Testament Christological hymns can be listed as follows: (1) Jesus is *of a divine state* in union with God, in a state of "equality"; (2) as God's Word, he is the *mediator of creation;* (3) at the same time, Jesus is *part of creation, God's incarnated agent* who descended from the heavenly to the earthly realm; (4) being part of creation, Jesus *lived, worked,* and *died;* (5) he was *made alive* again and *lives now;* (6) his life, work, death, and resurrection effects a *reconciliation* of

the world with God, brings creation to *fulfillment,* and *saves* the
world from sin; (7) Jesus, as the Christ and Lord, is now *exalted*
and *enthroned,* with the whole *cosmos subject to him.*[5]
   Each of these elements can be seen in the Pauline Christological hymns in Philippians, Colossians, and 1 Timothy. In Philippians Paul writes:

> For the divine nature was his from the first, yet he did
> not think to snatch at equality with God, but made him-
> self nothing, assuming the nature of a slave. Bearing the
> human likeness, revealed in human shape, he humbled
> himself, and in obedience accepted death—death on a
> cross. Therefore God raised him to the heights and be-
> stowed on him the name above all names, that at the
> name of Jesus every knee should bow—in heaven, on
> earth, and in the depths—and every tongue confess, "Je-
> sus Christ is Lord," to the glory of God the Father (Phil
> 2:6–11, *NEB*).

It is interesting to compare other translations of the first line
of this hymn. *The New English Bible* translation (*NEB*) noted
above reads: "For the *divine nature* was his from the first; yet he
did not think to *snatch* at equality with God. . . ." *The Jerusalem
Bible* (*JB*) reads: "His *state was divine* yet he did not *cling* to his
equality with God. . . ." *The Revised Standard Version* (RSV)
translates: "Though he was in the *form of God,* did not count
equality with God a thing to be grasped. . . ."
   What is noteworthy in this comparison of translations is that
each uses a different term to speak of Jesus' association with
God, and that each of these terms—"divine *nature,*" divine
"*state,*" "in the *form* of God"—when set in different philosophical
frameworks, could lead to different theological emphases. The intent of the hymn, however (captured in all of the translations), is
to celebrate the Christian belief that in the experience of Jesus is
the experience of God. Jesus proclaims *God-with-us*—God who
does not deign to dwell in the heavenly reaches or ask to be ap-
proached in fear and trembling, but rather seeks to dwell in human company. Jesus, who does not "snatch," "cling," or "grasp"
at divine glory, proclaims the *servant* and *suffering* God among
us.

In our second Christological hymn Paul sings:

He is the image of the unseen God
and the first-born of all creation,
for in him were created
all things in heaven and on earth:
everything visible and everything invisible,
Thrones, Dominations, Sovereignties, Powers—
all things were created through him and for him.
Before anything was created, he existed,
and he holds all things in unity.
Now the Church is his body,
he is its head.

As he is the Beginning
he was first to be born from the dead
so that he should be first in every way;
because God wanted all perfection
to be found in him
and all things to be reconciled through him and for him,
everything in heaven and everything on earth
when he made peace
by his death on the cross (Col 1:15–20, *JB*).

In this hymn Paul proclaims that it has pleased our Creator to dwell among us in Jesus, the reconciler of all creation, the maker of peace amid the terrors and violence of history, the sovereign over all heavenly and earthly powers, including the Church. All creation and powers in creation are subject to God "imaged" in Jesus the Christ. Any earthly claim to supremacy, whether intellectual, ecclesiastical, or political, is obscene in the sight of God and humankind.

Paul writes in our third Christological praise that "great beyond question is the mystery of our religion" (1 Tim 3:15, *NEB*):

He was manifested in the flesh,
vindicated in the spirit,
seen by angels,
preached among the nations,
believed on in the world,
taken up in glory (1 Tim 3:16, *RSV*).

Surely all theological explanations will pale in comparison to the height, width, and breadth of this mystery.

The Christological Hymn of John

From these early hymns of Paul our attention is drawn to the most familiar and perhaps the strongest of all New Testament Christological hymns—the Prologue of John's Gospel. As a later New Testament text, we find in the hymn of John the most intense concentration of basic Christological themes of the foundational Christian era—the Christology of Paul reconstructed in an eschatological, historical, and Greek philosophical mix. The high incarnational theology of John presents the man Jesus as the same pre-existent Word of God made flesh—the personification of wisdom and light, the Greek neo-Platonic Logos taken to new heights of divinization. Jesus, as the Word of God made flesh, is the *new* light to all nations, but a light "rejected" by his own people. Despite this rejection—and, in New Testament soteriology (theology of salvation), because of it—his light shines on in eschatological glory for all to see, "full of grace and truth." In the New Testament theology of salvation, the rejection of Jesus by institutional Judaism was the means to his suffering, death, and resurrection—the means of salvation. Tragically, however, the occasion for salvation, seen in light of Christianity's polemical rejection of its specific Judaic identity, would become in later history a cause of countless sufferings and deaths of Jews who could not follow the Christian way.

John's Christological hymn concludes with Peter's basic confession of Jesus Christ, the "only Son of the Father" (Jn 1:14 [*JB*]; 1–14). Of all the Christological titles, this is the most important because it has been the most influential and the most theologically problematic. It calls forth the greatest challenge for theological interpretation and signaled the final parting of the followers of Jesus from their religious home. The meaning of the phrase "Son of God"—the man Jesus' relation with God—both grounds the radical Christology of Christian faith and challenges its continuing claim to have remained monotheistic. What was and is a mystery of faith experience soon became—and continues to be—a problem for theological explanation.

The Title "Son of God"

Religious and Cultural Background

The title "Son of God" was not unknown in Jewish religion during the intertestamental period of Christian formation. It was used to indicate one who "belongs to the sphere of God."[6] Considering the patriarchal nature of the ancient Middle Eastern world, this masculine title *could* be applied to all just and righteous people who promoted God's cause in the world. The early Christian believers, however, used the title in a most extraordinary way when applied to Jesus. "Son of God" when used as a Christological title exhibited three basic characteristics:[7] (a) *pre-existence and intimate association with God*—a title of union and "equality with" God; (b) *one who is present at creation and the mediator of creation;* (c) *one who comes into the world as God's agent of wisdom and salvation.* And even though traditional Judaism would never intend such an identification of any or all of these characteristics with an historical person, vestiges of each can be found in various places in the Jewish religious and cultural heritage.

Jewish mysticism spoke of the unique and intimate association of the quasi-divine Metatron with God in the *Third Hebrew Book of Enoch.* Here, Enoch is caught up in a fiery heavenly ecstasy that transforms him into God's vizier and plenipotentiary.[8] In the apocalyptic Prayer of Joseph, Jacob-Israel is the personified incarnation of the power of the Lord "created before all the works of creation" and "descended incognito to earth."[9] It is in the nation of Jacob-Israel that salvation would come to the world.

Finally, the Jewish wisdom tradition, dating from the third century B.C.E., personifies wisdom as God's joyful companion before the creation of the world—"God's beloved child."[10] In Proverbs, Wisdom speaks:

When he marked out the foundations of the earth,
then I was beside him as his darling:
And I was daily his delight,
rejoicing before him always,
rejoicing in his inhabited world
and delighting in the sons of men (Prov 8:29–30, *JB*).

Wisdom is the mediator of God and world, finding rest in Jerusalem in the Torah, the word of God.[11] The Jewish-Greek philosopher and theologian Philo of Alexandria sees wisdom as the "daughter of God and the first-born mother of the universe."[12]

Philo assumes a great deal of importance for our understanding of the religious and philosophical background of New Testament Christology and for the interpretation of the meaning of the Christological title, "Son of God." He was a principal figure of the Hellenized Jewish diaspora which differed from Palestinian Judaism but was nonetheless influential upon it. Philo's unique combination of neo-Platonic philosophy and Jewish theology led to a more universalized form of systematic explanation that was more apt to bridge ethnic and territorial boundaries. Predating Paul by only one generation, Philonic thought met some of the universal interests of early Christianity and was undoubtedly an influence in New Testament theology. It is for Scripture scholars to determine how direct and to what degree that influence was, especially in the Christologies of Paul and John. But the fact cannot be denied that Greek philosophy in general, and Philonic thought in particular, was an influence in the New Testament and in the later Christological Councils of Nicea and Chalcedon.

Philo's neo-Platonic world was peopled with allegorical personifications of pure ideas and essences—pure forms that exhibited the essence of wisdom and truth experienced only as shadowy representations in the everyday world of human history. God, the purest of spiritual essences, and wisdom, the personification of the divine reason, are father and mother of the world. The great cosmic split between divine spirit and worldly matter is bridged in creation through the mediation of the Logos, the word of God as the first-born son of God's spirit. The created universe is the second son of father God and mother wisdom. Logos is God's ambassador in the world. Logos is "neither created nor uncreated." Only the Logos can make us "worthy of being called son of God through spiritual rebirth."[13] The divine word (Logos) and the divine reason (Wisdom) are present with God and in God from the beginning.[14] Creation's way back to God, the way from this shadowy, veiled world of representation and unreality—the way, in fact, of salvation—is (again in a phrase that is familiar to all readers of John's Prologue) through spiritual rebirth in the Logos. We hardly need to be reminded that in John's reconstruction this is the Word of God incarnate, Jesus, the Christ.

The Title "Son of God" in the New Testament

We can only briefly survey the use of the title "Son of God" in the Christology of the New Testament. Paul's early confession at the beginning of his Letter to the Romans is an appropriate place to start.[15]

> Paul, a servant of Jesus Christ, called to be an apostle, set apart for the gospel of God which he promised beforehand through his prophets in the holy scriptures, the gospel concerning his Son, who was descended from David according to the flesh and *designated Son of God in power according to the Spirit of holiness* by his resurrection from the dead, Jesus Christ our Lord . . . (Rom 1:1–4, *RSV*; emphasis added).

In this passage there is a flavor of Jesus' divine sonship by adoption and "designation"—sonship in the spirit of holiness. This same relatively "low Christology" (as opposed to the higher Christologies that stress pre-existence in a vertical model of incarnation by descent from above) is also found in the Synoptic accounts of Jesus' baptism. God speaks from the heavens in what could be construed as a *conferral* and *confirmation* of sonship: "This is my beloved Son, with whom I am well pleased" (Mt 3:17, *RSV*; see also Mk 1:11; Lk 3:22). I am sure that a debate exists among scriptural scholars about the meaning of these passages, but I at least am left to wonder whether these passages are indicating a conferral of divine sonship upon Jesus by God as a *task* as well as a *status*—a status to be attained when his task and mission are accomplished, culminating in his death and resurrection to new life. I will say more about the tendency of some Christologies to separate Jesus' status of Sonship from his mission and work in the later chapters.[16]

Even if we have indicated an early and less cosmic claim for Jesus' status of Sonship, we know that in Paul, John, and other places in the New Testament the notion will develop and grow under apocalyptic and eschatological influence. In Hebrews, for example, New Testament Christology clearly expresses a cosmic interpretation for the title "Son of God."[17] The letter opens with a declaration of the radical new word spoken to the followers of Jesus—that Jesus is Son of God, the inheritor of all things, the bearer of creation, the reflection of the glory of God "upholding the universe by his word of power" (Heb 1:1–3, RSV). Hebrews continues with the claim that the Sonship of Jesus raises him over the angels themselves and over all forms of spiritual persona or philosophically construed emanations: "For to what angel did God ever say, 'Thou art my Son, today I have begotten thee'?" (Heb 1:5, RSV). Jesus is Lord (Kyrios) who "found the earth in the beginning," and who created the heavens as "the work of thy hands" (Heb 1:10, RSV).[18]

We can conclude our brief examination of the title "Son of God" in the New Testament by turning to the writings of John. Toward the end of the first century C.E. in the last period of New Testament writing, John presents a summary and a climax of biblical Christology.[19] The same pre-existent divine Word, the mediator of creation made flesh as the light of salvation, is the same Jesus of Nazareth, the only Son of God given to the world so that the world would not perish but have life[20] (see Jn 1:1–16). The words of Jesus are now taken as those of the cosmic Lord of heaven and earth revealed in John's mystical vision as "the words of the Son of God, who has eyes like a flame of fire, and whose feet are like burnished bronze" (Rev 2:18, RSV).

THE CHRISTOLOGICAL PARADOX AND THE THEOLOGICAL PROBLEM

Despite the variety of Christological emphases in the era of Christian establishment, New Testament theology does not utilize the title "Son of God" as an allegorical personification but rather as an historical identification. The Son of God is the same Jesus of Nazareth who walked among us.[21] For the followers of Jesus, their experience of him in the flesh seen in light of faith was the experience of God. He was and is God's Son and Lord of the universe. He is the herald of the end-time and the hope for the fulfillment of future-time. He is the "first-born of all creation," existing with God "in the beginning." However, the same faith also confessed throughout the New Testament writings that his "equality" with God, his status as cosmic Lord, was given up for us. He came in the flesh as *God-with-us* and died in the flesh as *God's pledge to us.*

This mixture of divine and human motifs in New Testament Christology—Jesus' oneness with God and his familiarity with us—created a paradox at the very foundation of Christian faith.[22] How could the belief in his divine status and the fact of his human reality be interrelated? Since faith-mysteries were total envelopments of self and life—by their nature *supra*-rational—the Christian confession could absorb this paradox. Developing Christian theology, however, could not so easily absorb mysterious paradoxes but instead transformed them into problems for rational solution.[23] The Christological problem of interrelating the divine and the human in the Christian confession of Jesus as the Christ, the "Son of the living God," would occupy the Church for the next three centuries after its foundational era and, indeed, for every century thereafter.

Chapter III
PARADOX AND PROBLEM

THE CHRISTOLOGICAL PARADOX AS
A THEOLOGICAL PROBLEM

The Basic Paradox Reviewed

I have argued that at the heart of New Testament Christology a basic paradox is expressed in a number of forms. Jesus, the Christ, is at one and the same time of earth and heaven; he is worthy of exaltation yet chose humiliation. He proclaimed the divine reaffirmation of salvation for an undeserving, sinful world. He is the expression of both the transcendence and the immanence of God—God in cosmic glory, God in mortal flesh. This Christological paradox is rooted in the more general paradox of all theistic faith—the infinite God's involvement in the finite world in general and in the even more finite worlds of individual personal lives. Yet the New Testament's confession of Jesus as the only Son of God is perhaps the most radically paradoxical faith of all theistic religion. The God of power and glory, of majesty and mystery, is most intensely present in the world in the person of an itinerant rabbinic teacher crucified by the Roman governor of Palestine for disturbing the public order.

Modeling the Paradox

When the first followers of Jesus grew in their own self-understanding to the point of confessing this most radical and paradoxical faith, they were challenged to find initial models for its rational articulation. Their own faith experience needed to be expressed and proclaimed. In order to do this, the paradox had to be *modeled,* as it were—presented in some initial coherent pattern. This modeling was the burden of New Testament Christology and the continuing challenge for all Christological developments since that time.

Theological Modeling: The Method of Imagination

The adaptation of conceptual models for describing and explaining faith experiences is the core of theological method. Initial theological models are drawn of necessity from the cultural milieu of any given era. Models that seem best to capture fundamental faith experiences and basic confessions, though always limited, survive and form part of a theological tradition. Some models pass away because their cultural underpinning loses its meaning; others are judged inadequate as explanations of faith. Still others survive in institutional religion long after cultural changes have rendered them ungrounded; such models, even though now archaic, are supported because of confusion about what is to count as fidelity and/or because of their usefulness for the stability of religious institutions.

The necessity of theological modeling of faith experience and confession arises from the nature of theology as secondary and indirect discourse. If, as I have argued, it is the faith experience which always assumes a temporal and phenomenal priority in religious life—the priority of a "happening" or an event of interpersonal confrontation and commitment—then theological articulations are always secondary commentaries on that experience. At the same time, faith events confront both self and other at levels of deep human experience that transcend the ordinary limits of functional daily life. The attempt of theological modeling to capture such "limit-experiences"[1] creates a mode of indirect speech that necessarily involves analogical, metaphorical, and mythic language. Since theological discourse cannot capture the depth of faith experience, its modeling and speech must rely on concepts and phrases that can only *image* that experience in some symbolic way. The building of theological models is in fact an *exercise of* our rational and artistic *imagination.*[2] We can only "imagine" ways to speak of transcending experiences; we can never describe them directly.

The analogy between faith and love is again suggestive. Just as those who wish to describe the experience of love need to utilize symbols, metaphors, stories and songs, theological discourse must appeal in a similar way to the constructive imagination. God, God's Word, the Christ as Son of God are all theological phrases which are initial attempts to name deep experiences of life and faith; such phrases are never simply and objectively descriptive as are observations of simple realities for all to see. Like all constructive theology, New Testament Christology is marked by its attempt to construct imaginative models that offer an initial framework for understanding the basic Christian paradox.

It would be incorrect to think that imaginative discourse in theology or in art is necessarily false discourse. On the contrary, at levels of transcendent and transcending experience, it is the only kind of speech that has any real hope of being true. The tendency to objectivize transcending experiences like faith and love—the tendency to offer what can count as quasi-scientific proof—needs to be overcome if we are to understand religious experience in general and the New Testament experience in particular. Even though religious experience is transcending, it is not "out of this world." In this sense "transcendent" means "going beyond" the ordinary and everyday modes of functional existence, coming to heights and depths of insight and experience that are revelatory of the root meanings of our lives *in the world.*

New Testament Christological Models

We now need to attend to the basic Christological models formed by the New Testament writers as they exercised their own constructive theological imagination. I am not suggesting that the following types are exhaustive. They are, however, the ones that initially come to mind—that seem to stand out as major coordinating patterns for New Testament Christology. As we have seen, the imaginative constructions of New Testament theology drew from the more general religious and cultural imaginations of its time—reconstructing existing images in light of its own radical question. "Who do you say that I am?" is in fact a transcendental question that probes well beyond one's biological nature or socio-economic role. Questions of personal identity, whether we ask them of ourselves or of others, are deep probes which take us beyond surface realities. Such questions always require imaginative constructions of our philosophical and, for "believers," our religious and theological imaginations.

We have already noted the existence of apocalyptic and eschatological themes in the New Testament era. Apocalyptic and eschatological movements always imply a soteriology—a theme of salvation from the terrors, dreaded fate, and sins of human history. Jesus, as the Christ, proclaimed for his followers the day of the Lord God—the end of all former ways of life and the advent of the time of fulfillment for both self and world. In order to answer the question of the identity of this man who would bring such a universal new creation, New Testament Christology began the task of theological modeling.

Because the task of salvation was cosmic as well as personal, dealing with the reconciliation of the whole universe as the "new creation," New Testament Christology presented a certain cosmological framework for identifying Jesus. If one could be located in the basically three-tiered cosmos of heaven, earth, and "under the earth," then one's place in reference to God's created order would give the identity sought. We noticed such cosmological motifs in both the Pauline Christological hymns and in John's Prologue: the Word of God located from the beginning with God; descending to earth, incarnated as Jesus of Nazareth; crucified, died, descended to the nether world and resurrected, ascends to reassume his rightful place as Lord. We also noted in this cosmological model a notion of divine generation of Jesus as Son of God—a metaphor of biological sonship taken to cosmological proportions.

Along with the overriding cosmological Christology of the New Testament, there also exists a more earth-centered moral model. Jesus is the Christ and Lord because of his radical fidelity to God and to the accomplishment of God's work and God's will. Jesus' identity is seen in his religious and moral union with his "Father in heaven." The Father has designated the Son to bring the good news of salvation, to preach and to act out that news even unto death. Instead of a metaphor of cosmological generation, Jesus' sonship is one of interpersonal fidelity, of a loving and intimate union.

It is certainly true that even though I have distinguished between cosmological emphases and more earth-centered moral ones in New Testament Christology, the two are often intermingled. During the largest part of the Christian era, I would venture to say that the cosmological models have been the most dominant. They also seem to dominate in the New Testament, perhaps because of a pre-scientific, mythic cosmology or because in this foundational period they seemed to present a stronger claim than the more earth-bound moral models. Creator God ruled the heavens, the earth, and all under the earth with power and majesty. There was no basic change by the Christians in this core truth of Jewish religion. Cosmological Christology opted to reconstruct its model of Jesus the Christ around this basic creation theme rather than the more subtle and, indeed, less flamboyant model of internal moral fidelity.

The final Christological model to be emphasized in fact combines cosmological motifs with moral ones in the basic Christian paradox of exaltation and humiliation. The pre-existent Word of God is the same Jesus of Nazareth who preached and worked among us, died for us, and rose in glory to bring salvation to a troubled world. This Christian soteriological model (model of salvation) is, as I have argued, the unifying Christological theme running throughout the New Testament. Therefore, even with the initial attempts of New Testament Christology at modeling its faith experience and confession in some rational way, the basic Christological paradox remained.

Addressing the Paradox as a Theological Problem

The basic difference between the New Testament Christological models and those that were to immediately follow was the emphasis attached to each side of the polar relationship between faith and theology. In one way or another, the New Testament writers were primarily witnesses of faith in Jesus. For them, the faith experience and its confession were primary. Their writings were oriented toward giving a foundational testimony—their *new testament*—to belief in Jesus as the Christ, the Son of the living God. Their basic challenge was to sort out what was normative from among the plurality of primary articulations of faith. This is not to say that there were not initial theological conflicts even in this foundational era. It is to say, however, that during this time theological articulation was seen as a servant of the faith experience. It seems clear that there is more confession in the New Testament than theological sophistication or expertise. Theological experts did not write these testaments. They were penned instead by committed people taken up in what they perceived to be the dramatic apex of human history itself—a history that was either fast coming to its end (apocalyptic) or at least had experienced the one who imaged its final fulfillment: Jesus, the "first-born of creation," the "alpha" and the "omega," the beginning and the end (eschatological).

In such a milieu of high transcendental drama, paradoxes were required. The drama of the apex of time and history itself could not be described in simply direct speech. God's word had been spoken and had appeared. Whatever could be confessed and said about this Word of God—Jesus—would of necessity have the paradoxical flavor of the best high drama. Thus, the theological models adopted in the New Testament were neither highly philosophical nor systematic. The demand was not for logical coherence but for dramatic effect—to draw its audience into the experience of faith. Since the early followers of Jesus had no social or political power and did not initially seek such power, their faith and theology could remain simple for a time—at the level of preaching and witness. The moral dangers of corrupting power would come later; inevitably, as Christians become more socially and politically successful, the followers were institutionalized as a Church.

The formulation of the *sociological* entity of a Church has always been considered somewhat an ambiguity by many Christian believers. They long for the simple confessions of faith with only enough theology for initial coherence. Yet at the same time, they realize that the complexities of survival of a doctrine having universal religious and moral intent demands institutionalization with all of its attendant strengths and weaknesses. In this movement toward institutionalization, the delicate balance between faith and theology began to shift in the Christian Church. At least in the upper echelons, the now-organized schools of theological intelligentsia began to develop in such a way that the shift of emphasis moved in the favor of theology. Expertise of theological formulation, conceptual clarification, and logical systematization began to be emphasized in a way not precedented in the New Testament. To be sure, the New Testament models were still considered foundational in these systematizations, but their functional role as servants of faith shifted. Fidelity was no longer primarily the confession of Jesus as "the Christ, the Son of the living God," but now meant also (and even primarily) conformity to standard theological explanations. *Fidelity, in short, came to mean orthodoxy.*

The Christological *paradox* so essential for describing the experience of high faith-drama of the early followers of Jesus now became a theological *problem* that sought consistent and standardized explanations. There was no lack of surface drama in the Christological debates of the early Church councils (even "high" drama when theological explanation was confused with faith), but the paradigm had shifted. New Testament Christology had lost some of its characterization as a dramatic play whose script told of cosmic and personal struggles for truth and right, for salvation from human terror and death, and for the victory of the reign of God in the world. What had been essentially an existential participation in the play of human history to a large degree became a logical, philosophical struggle for rational ascendancy—the victory of one theological theory over another.

Again, I want to emphasize that even in the era of great Christological debate in the fourth century, New Testament faith and its initial theological models were foundational concerns. However, my thesis is that there was a shift in emphasis from the priority of faith to that of theology and institutional cohesiveness. That this shift was to some extent necessary and these concerns to some extent legitimate does not take away a sense of regret over the loss of the dramatic intensity of the New Testament era. Nor does the fact that these Christological debates seemed for many like defenses of the faith remove the underlying confusion between faith and theology inherent in the notion of theological orthodoxy itself. Some of the power of the Christological paradox had been diluted in its tranformation into a theological problem.

It is important to pause and recall our reflections on the relationship between faith and theology. We have noted that faith without theology is blind and can commit its share of errors. As attractive as the commitment of the early followers of Jesus may be, or as sincere as the faith of latter witnesses remains, other religious traditions were and continue to be negated. Theological expertise, however, runs its own risk of serving mainly elitist academic interests or institutional interests in conformity and functional efficiency. Even though all organizations—religions included—need some standardization, overriding functionalist orientations always run the risk of stifling initiative and creative plurality. If left unchecked, such institutional functionalism will wreak havoc on all non-conformists both within and without the standardized system.

The Church of the fourth century was still a new organization; some standardization was necessary. But the paradigmatic shift from the primacy of faith to theology and the confusion of confessional fidelity with theological orthodoxy and, indeed, with socio-political conformity was in the long run not only a loss for the Christian Church but also the basic ground for its tragic history of the persecution of Jews.

BUILDING CHRISTOLOGICAL DOCTRINE AND DOGMA

Conflicting Doctrines

The principal theological problem with the Christological paradox of the New Testament, at least in terms of Christianity's own religious heritage, was the challenge to remain monotheistic. Had Christian faith claimed too much? How could monotheism and New Testament Christology be reconciled? Despite any and all theological problems, monotheism was a requisite for Christian faith. Whatever else Jesus claimed to be, whatever else his followers proclaimed him to be, he was first and last a monotheistic Jew. In his history of the Christian Church, Paul Johnson summarizes the theological tensions of the post-New Testament era as Christianity re-examined its new self-identity in light of the radical separation from its Jewish heritage:

In the first century the world was waiting for a monotheistic, universalistic religion. Christianity supplied it. But then: Was Christianity truly monotheistic? In the last resort what distinguished it from Judaism was belief in the divinity of Christ. If Jesus were a mere messiah then the two religious systems were reconcilable, as indeed Jewish Christians had argued. But insistence that Jesus was the son of God placed the movement right outside even the furthest confines of Judaic thought and not only separated the systems but brought them into moral enmity. This situation was in time brought about by the victory of Pauline theology. The divinity of Christ gave Christianity its tremendous initial impact and assisted its universality. But it left Christian theologians with a dilemma: how to explain the divinity of Christ while maintaining the singularity of God. Were there not two Gods? Or, if the concept of the Spirit were introduced as a separate manifestation of divinity, three?[3]

The Foundations of Christological Dogma

In the two centuries following the New Testament era, a multitude of theological questions and answers emerged as this fundamental dilemma was addressed. What the New Testament failed to systematize in any developed way became the task for the growing body of professional Christian scholars and theologians. How is Jesus the Christ the Son of the living God? What in fact *is* the relationship between the divine and the human—between God and creation focused in Jesus? Are spirit and flesh compatible or antagonistic? If compatible, is not flesh merely the medium through which the glory of God shines through? If incompatible, what are we to make of Jesus' suffering and death? Was his human quality—his suffering and death—merely an appearance? And finally, if Jesus is *joined in God*—the mediator between God and the world—are we to say that he is *identified with God?*

We cannot discuss in any detail the multiplicity of doctrinal Christologies that emerged during this period. Even an abbreviated listing of various schools of thought leads to the inescapable conclusion of theological pluralism and conflict. *Docetism* emphasized the divinity of the Christ and taught that the sufferings and death of Jesus were only appearances. *Nestorianism* stressed the humanity of Jesus to such an extent that it was led to deny the popular faith that Mary was the mother of God (the *Theotokos*). *Monarchianism* taught that there could be no sharp distinctions in the unity of God and presented an anti-Trinitarian Christology. *Modalism*, and later *Sabellianism*, stressed that all Trinitarian models were descriptions of God's activity in the world and not subject to metaphysical discrimination.[4] These and other Christologies of later centuries alternated in their stress on each side of the Christological paradox: divinity and humanity, exaltation and humiliation. In one way or another all of them attempted to combine their own understandings of the New Testament confession (or their own selective part of it) with the more systematic Greek and Roman philosophical systems.

However, the first major doctrinal conflict—major because its resolution set the foundation for Christian *dogma*—was initiated by the teaching of the Alexandrian priest, Arius. In many ways Arius tried to present a mixed Christological model that intended to uphold Christian monotheism while at the same time presenting a unique and cosmic place for Jesus in God's scheme of salvation. What we know of Arianism can only be gleaned from the writings of his opponents. He seemed to say that only God can be unbegotten as infinite and eternal. Since the Son of God—God's Word made flesh in Jesus—proceeds from God, he is in fact less than God. The *logic* of procession led to a status of inferiority in being—"there was a time when the Son was not."[5] As Logos, however, the Son of God is not like other creatures but is rather the intermediate point of contact between God and the world—a quasi-divine and quasi-human being.[6]

The Arian debate was at one and the same time a theological and political controversy. Many, if not most, of the upper echelons of Church life during the early fourth century were essentially Arian in their Christology. The lower echelons, along with the faithful, were not. The Greek (Saint) Athanasius led the fight for condemnation of Arianism. The Roman emperor, Constantine, with his interest in peaceful compromise, pushed for resolution.

The Church Council of Nicea in 325 C.E. condemned Arian Christology as heretical and presented its own theological statement as orthodox and standard. Jesus the Christ is "true God from true God, *one essence or being* with the Father."[7] This statement, preserved in Christian life as the core of the Nicean or Athanasian Creed, was both a theological and political compromise. The key phrase, "one essence in being" (*homoousion* in Greek and proposed by the emperor[8]), was philosophically abstract enough to satisfy the majority, at least for the time being. It also overcame Arius' unfortunate attempt to "split the difference," as it were, in the paradigmatic Christological paradox. Arius interpreted a Christology that hung between heaven and earth. His basically correct interest in upholding monotheistic faith led to a portrait of Christ that did not satisfy the paradoxical Christian confession. Jesus was neither true God nor true man. Arius tried to collapse the paradox and render it irrelevant. The wisdom of Athanasius and Constantine was to deny the Arian hybrid while postponing the remaining theological question. However, if Jesus is "one essence in being" with the Father, how is he human? This question would remain until addressed again later in the fifth century by the most important Christological Council of Chalcedon.

That the question was not resolved was indicated by the reinstatement of Arius, the banishment of Athanasius, and the attempts of Arian thought to find more acceptable theological terminology to explain the Christ's relation to God (the chief of which was *homoiousion*—"like in essential being"). Athanasius' "staying power," however, was not to be discounted. He was returned to favor, Arius was banished again, and Nicean orthodoxy was upheld at the First Council of Constantinople in 381.[9]

The Council of Chalcedon: Completing the Standard Dogma

The Council of Chalcedon in 451 C.E. reaffirmed the teaching of the Councils of Nicea and Constantinople and presented a Christological model that would become standard for the intervening fifteen centuries to the present day. Starting in the nineteenth century, certain reconstructions of the Chalcedon model have been and are still being attempted. However, Chalcedon remains in the background, causing as many theological difficulties as it solved. Some contemporary theologians wonder whether the Chalcedon model has now become archaic and ought to be retired as part of Christian antiquity. A word of warning is in order: a model of such duration, no matter how reconstructed, has for good and for bad become part of the Christian tradition. *Our challenge is to retain its wisdom and mitigate as far as possible its weaknesses.*

Chalcedonian Christology

The decree of the Council of Chalcedon can be excerpted as follows with a notation of the hyphenated character of its own Christological model: Jesus is at one and the same time God and human, the "God-man."

> Following, therefore, the holy fathers, we confess one and the same Son, who is our Lord Jesus Christ, and we all agree in teaching ... the same—in his humanity, *truly God* and *truly a human* being, this very same one being composed of a rational soul and body, *co-essential with the Father* as to his deity and *co-essential with us— the very same one*—as to his humanity, being like us in every respect apart from sin. As to his deity, he was born from our Father before all ages, but as to his humanity, *the very same one* was born in the last days from the Virgin Mary, the Mother of God, for our sake and the sake of salvation: *one and the same* Christ, Son, Lord, Only Begotten, acknowledged to be *unconfusedly, unalterably, undividedly, inseparably in two natures,* since the difference of natures is not destroyed because of this union, but on the contrary, *the character of each nature is preserved and comes together in one person* and *one hypostasis, not divided* or torn *into two persons* but *one and the same Son* and only-begotten God, Logos, Lord Jesus Christ.[10]

The decree ends by a now rather common statement of its intentions to provide the standard orthodox Christological statement. What it sees to be the threats to orthodoxy, however, are indicated by its particular references:

> Those who dare to compose another creed or to bring forward or teach or transmit another symbol to people who want to turn to the knowledge of truth from Helle-

nism or Judaism or from any heresy whatever—such persons, if they are bishops or clergy, are deposed . . . if they are monks or laity they are anathematized.[11]

The Strengths and Weaknesses of Chalcedonian Christology

The basic strength and wisdom of Chalcedon's hyphenated Christology is its intention to uphold the basic Christological paradox and present it in a bi-polar theological model. Unlike Arius who tried to present a theological hybrid (a Christ in mid-air, so to speak), Chalcedon says that Jesus is bi-natured, maintained in an hypostasis of one person. This is the core *hypostatic union* of Chalcedonian Christology—a metaphysical union of distinct natures in one person (as opposed to a moral union of wills with God[12]—a union of fidelity and love). Chalcedon "solves" the problem of divine spirit and human flesh by separating them into two natures and then rejoining what has been separated in a mystical unity of person. The terms of the Christological paradox are thus retained, but a model for explanation is provided that maintains the singular identity of Jesus the Christ.

There are several weaknesses in the Chalcedonian declaration. First, the model is centered in a rather tortured philosophical construct for which there are no clear analogies in human metaphors. Theological constructions of this kind always run the risk of being finally more mystifying than explanatory. It seems to be true that the Chalcedonian model requires as much philosophical "faith" in the phenomenon of an *hypostasis* of two natures in one person as it does religious faith in Jesus as the Christ.

Second, even if we can attain such a faith in a now-archaic philosophical system, the Chalcedonian declaration does not finally tell us how such an hypostasis is effected.[13] With an esoteric philosophical construction, it binds itself to the defense of that construction as well as a defense of the faith being modeled. Even though this systematization was not the intent of the final declaration, Chalcedon's theological model was bound to its systematic philosophical foundation with all of its strengths and weaknesses. This is not a unique problem to this model, but one which inheres in all philosophically oriented systematic theology. Chalcedon's problem (and the problem for all non-conformists) was compounded when in effect its faith declaration and inherent theological-philosophical formulation were *both* declared ortho-dox.

This brings us to the third weakness of Chalcedonian Christology, its claim to orthodoxy. Orthodoxy means precisely "right belief" (or right opinion). However, it was used at Nicea and Chalcedon (and thereafter) to mean the normative and standard teaching of particular groups.[14] The problem with orthodoxy is related to the above demand for a philosophical as well as religious faith. Despite the necessity for some basic confessional and theological standards for the self-identity of any institution, when those standards are too strict and the range of options too narrow, theological models begin to replace faith as the object of fidelity. When cast in this way, orthodoxy canonizes what must always remain plural and capable of correction and reconstruction—namely, the theological models of faith.

THE DANGERS OF THEOLOGICAL MONISM

The "triumph" of orthodoxy and the "failure" of heresy in the Christological debates of the fourth and fifth centuries led the Church into a rather dangerous tradition of theological monism—dangerous to the vitality of its own internal life and dangerous for all those anathematized because of their non-conformity. This is not to say that claims of orthodoxy are sinister in themselves or that pluralities of theological models are always signs of vitality. The problem arises, as I have argued, when the promotion of systematic theological orthodoxy and its attendant philosophical foundation replace the primacy of fidelity—an orthodoxy of faith.

Thus, the "triumph" of Christological orthodoxy and the "failure" of Christological "heresy" at Nicea and Chalcedon led to a certain hesitation on the part of the Church to engage in the ongoing task of finding new, more creative theological models for the Christian faith. While it is true that other "heresies" emerged after Chalcedon (the most important of which was Monophysitism's denial of the two-nature dogma[15]), its Christology was standard, surviving in virtually all Christian denominations.

This entrenchment of Christology around a singular model only intensified the call for conformity and the rejection of difference. Judaism's continuing rejection of any and all Christological confessions and models was only the most extreme example of this non-conformity. The Church's own internal struggles in the polarization of theological orthodoxy and theological heresy in fact reinforced its continuing tradition of the negation of Judaism.

It may be appropriate to make a brief point about the value of functional "heresy"—those non-conformist theological models and formulations that are part and parcel of the function of theological reconstruction and imagination. Again, I am not arguing that all non-orthodox formulations are equally engaging and valuable. Some of the classical "heresies" were stranger in their constructions than either Nicea or Chalcedon. However, I am supporting the value of freedom in the Church for the function of our theological imagination, always rooted in the constructive interest of enhancing the faith and in the critical moral interest of promoting a kingdom of justice and peace in the world. Thus, what can count as "functional heresy"—models not in conformity with mainline Christological tradition—is necessary if the Church is to retain a vital and open theological imagination. This sense of openness and, indeed, of respect for the mystery of God and God's involvement with the world—the mystery of Jesus Christ himself—will aid the Church in overcoming its own prideful sense of *possessing* the truth and its tragic tradition of persecuting those claimed *not* to possess it.

CHRISTOLOGICAL REINTERPRETATION AND RECONSTRUCTION

General Notions for a Critical-Interpretive Method

My thesis throughout has been that reinterpreting and reconstructing Christological models is both possible and necessary. The basic phenomenon of faith, the nature of theological discourse, and the fundamental relationship between the two make such reinterpretation and reconstruction possible. The Church's constant need for "new life," along with its tragic heritage of negating and persecuting non-conformists both within and without its boundaries, makes it religiously and morally necessary. I can only present a bare outline of what I think an adequate method of reinterpretation and reconstruction ought to be.[16]

At the outset, our attention must be drawn to the challenge of living within a tradition of faith and theology: *"living within"* is the key term. We are confronted by the demands of both vitality and fidelity to recall our past traditions, to bring them to new life by reinterpreting them in the present, and finally to reconstruct our tradition as a vital heritage to pass on to the future. Fidelity does not mean merely restating in the same way what we have received as tradition. The religious and theological constructions of our past were themselves historically situated in time and place. They were responses to both general and particular question of deep human meaning. Thus, as far as possible we must reconstruct the question addressed before we can understand the response given. We have noticed that much of our Christological tradition was formulated as particular responses to questions that either do not presently engage or ought not to engage us—for example, the negation of Jewish religion as an aid to new self-identity. At the same time, in the background of our Christological tradition are also basic and perennial inquiries into the meaning of human life itself. These questions are still with us and have the same urgency experienced by our forebears. Therefore, any reinterpretation is first a sorting-out process. What questions are still pertinent and of transhistorical significance, asking what in fact it means to be human in the world?

After this process of initial reconstruction, we must then bring our own specific inquiries—those rooted in our own historical time and circumstance—to what we have received as tradition. The perennial questions that we ask are flavored by our own placement in time and history—by our own world of daily affairs, our own particular fears and dreads, and our own experience of being human in the world. Even though the form of the questions may be the same, the milieu of inquiry, the way in which they emerge, and the symbolic constructions of our answers will be somewhat different. We should get some small consolation from realizing that some form of reinterpretation and reconstruction is part and parcel of the human search for meaning: it was most certainly a root phenomenon in the New Testament writing and in all imaginative attempts of religions and theological language. Such

tasks are resisted only at our peril—peril to our own vitality and
morality.

New Testament Christology

The New Testament era was a mixture of general questions
about human meaning as well as questions specific to that particular place and time. As always when dealing with ancient traditions, we thus have questions and responses that pertain to us
and those that do not—or do so only insofar as understanding
them will aid us in the necessary sorting-out process of reinterpretation and reconstruction. It is simply no longer adequate to
maintain monolithic views of the New Testament or of theological
notions like inspiration and revelation. The inspiration of the
New Testament and its revelation involve its raising and attempting to answer universal questions of meaning: Who are we? How
did we come to be? Why are we here? How are we to behave?
What is our destiny? How are we to be saved from tragic fate?
    That all of these questions were answered with reference to
Jesus, the mediator of the radically monotheistic God to us and us
to God, is the paradigmatic confession of all Christians. Hans
Küng presents a short description of a Christian as one who confesses that in all matters of life and death Jesus Christ is ultimately decisive.[17] I suspect that as insightful as such a description
might be, Christians must say more. In short, we must answer Jesus' own question of identity: "Who do *you* say that I am?" Christians believe that Jesus the Christ is ultimately decisive because
he is the "Son of the living God." His union with God and with us
is part of our normative confession. How any Christian, including
the New Testament writers, goes about explaining such a union
is, I suggest, always influenced by our own theological imagination and the theological model we use.
    The New Testament theological models are not in my view
part of its unique revelation. That Jesus is in union with God, that
he is *the* revelation of God in the world and the mediator of the
world's presence to God, *is* part of the normative Christian faith.
We may use terms like "equality" and "unity" with God, and
(even though rarely used in the New Testament) terms that depict
an identity with God. The Christian testaments certainly say

these things and more. But it says them primarily in *confessional* ways—ways that search for adequate metaphors and symbols for identifying Jesus as the Christ, the Son of God. Such terms are always set in some system of explanation. However, these systems and their implied definitions of terms change with history and culture and will therefore remain plural.

A note is necessary here about how the New Testament itself views the status of its own claims for Jesus. There is no question that these writers believed their Christological claims to be true; so too must Christians. As we have seen, however, it is a truth finally rooted in existential encounters of faith rather than in quasi-scientific demonstrations of some sort of *external* objective reality. All of the miracle stories of the New Testament and even the resurrection should be seen in this context. Even though the rhetoric surrounding the miracle stories has a flavor of scientific demonstration, their fundamental role is to proclaim a faith that has cosmic significance. In the cosmological Christological model of an ancient, pre-scientific (in a modern sense) world, it was only consistent to present the faith in Jesus in terms of universal power over nature. At the same time, all miracles—*especially the resurrection*—function in the New Testament more profoundly as signifiers of basic religious and moral truths. They point to insights into the meaning of human life; they manifest the deeper significance that interpersonal interaction through the spirit of love transcends all natural and physical phenomena, even our fated death.

Doctrinal/Dogmatic Christological Tradition

When we come to the challenge of reinterpreting Christological doctrine and dogma as it developed in the Church's historical tradition, we must apply our same methods. In one sense, the challenge of reinterpretation and reconstruction has grown more complex because of the intrusion of institutional and political interests; yet in another sense it is less complex, since the philosophical systems underlying the doctrines and dogmas are more easily identified. The strong Christology of identification of Jesus with God and the union of dual natures in one person are in these eras clearly based on philosophical formulations and systems not *developed* in the New Testament. This in itself does not make them inappropriate or wrong. It does, however, indicate that the theological method of modeling has been a consistent one in the Church, and that when we engage in it today, we are not doing something foreign or strange, much less unfaithful. We will create new models to the extent that the older ones have lost their meaning and their ability to enhance the faith in a modern world. What in fact are we to make today of mystifying theological words such as homoousion or "hypostatic union?" Do we view the world any longer through this sort of Greek philosophical eye? Is our Christology wedded to such formulations? Does fidelity to New Testament faith demand it? At the same time, we must be wary not to canonize our own new imaginative Christological models, instead always gauging them by the insight that God and God's ways with the world—God's manifestation and union in Jesus the Christ—are first and foremost *mysteries* that encompass us rather than theological problems that can finally be solved.

TRENDS IN CONTEMPORARY CHRISTOLOGY

Contemporary Christology generally exhibits a number of basic trends and interests.[18] As it developed over the centuries, the hyphenated Christology of Chalcedon led to an absorption of Jesus' humanity by the notion of divinity. The "hyphen," in short, was so diluted that Jesus was presented as atypically human at least and superhuman at most. In either event, he was very much unlike us. The new Christologies, with their renewed emphasis on a recombination of Jesus' work and mission with his own identity as the Christ, have attempted to reconstruct an adequate notion of his humanity which is essential for Christian faith.[19] Cosmological models have been understandably replaced with more morally oriented, interrelational ones. Contemporary Christologies search for symbols and metaphors existing in our own world view and experience of life with each other to explain Christian faith—something that is no longer possible with the ancient cosmological orientations. Such approaches bring Christology "downstage," so to speak, and recover its essential roots[20] in the struggles of every man and woman for *meaning* and *salvation* in the world. Our theological imagination, in short, must now be directed toward models that speak to our relationships and experiences *in this world.* We no longer look to the starry heavens for metaphors and models for meaning: now we look mainly into the depths of ourselves and our interrelationships with others.

The mythic cosmology of the New Testament and early Christian world was intended to function in quite the same way—to give insight into the world of daily living. We are simply looking for this same insight by using different metaphors, symbols, and models that are more relevant for us and faithful to our own searches for religious meaning, theological vitality, and moral responsibility. For Christians, Jesus is *still* the "Christ," *still* the "Son of the living God," *still* "ultimately decisive in all matters of life and death."

To be a Christian today must mean an affirmation of all sincere seekers of truth and right—those who speak of God and those who do not, all who promote God's cause of peace and justice in the world. Despite all the power, grace, and truth of confessions of faith in Jesus and of all Christological formulations old and new, if Christianity continues to engage in prideful dogmatism and immoral negations, it will lose its own soul—a soul it believes to have been infused by the grace of God made present in Jesus Christ.

Contemporary Christology will not create a situation of basic religious reunion with Judaism. Despite the modifications and reconstructions of traditional Christology, the emphasis must remain on the centrality of Jesus Christ as the mediating presence of God and world—the incarnation of the divine presence in the life of this human person. Incarnation is indeed set in a less cosmological and spatial notion of "descent from above," but the sacramental character of finding the one God among us, around us, and within us—the God "of flesh" and "in flesh," "living, suffering, dying and being reborn again," the mysterious Christian paradox of exaltation and humiliation, divinity and humanity—remains normative.

Judaism reminds Christianity that its faith remains paradoxical, that it is no small matter to speak of the transcendant God in such corporeal terms, that its Christology will always be problematic for monotheistic faith, that the messianic reign of peace and justice is not in place,[21] and that Christological triumphalism is out of place amid the horrors of twentieth century inhumanity. Christianity must remind itself and all those whom it contacts that its faith and theology can be respectful yet powerful, that the Christian paradox has wisdom to offer the world, that it can be again (as it has always been for some) a source of comfort and salvation and a continuing reincarnation of the true spirit of Jesus the Christ.

The primacy and the centrality of the Christian paradox as the character of its faith and the foundation of its theology is expressed succinctly and beautifully by the theologian Paul Tillich. The emphasis I have added highlights at the same time a faithful and respectful posture for Christians to take toward non-Christians:

> *We only want to communicate* to you *an experience* we have had that *here and there* in the world and *now and then* in ourselves is *a New Creation, usually hidden,* but *sometimes manifest,* and *certainly manifest in Jesus* who is called *the Christ.*[22]

Chapter IV
NOTES FOR
A RECONSTRUCTED
CHRISTOLOGY

INTRODUCTION

This essay in Christian-Jewish dialogue would be incomplete without at least some preliminary attention to the actual task of reconstructing a non-negating Christology—one that does not renounce Judaism or any other non-Christian religion at the outset as a viable search for God. At the same time, if this task is to be taken up with a constructive intention of enhancing Christian faith, such a Christology must be subject to norms of truthfulness and fidelity as well as moral norms of right and good. What follows can be no more than an outline of notes—initial suggestions for further dialogue both within and without the Christian houses of faith.

I will begin with a brief summary of the norms of adequacy for any reconstructed Christology: norms of truth, right and good, and fidelity. Then we will discuss initial and core theological notes followed by a critical examination of foundational interpretations for a new Christology. Finally, I will suggest what must serve as a bare outline for a Christological model that attempts to satisfy the preceding norms, notes, and interpretations.

NORMS FOR AN ADEQUATE CHRISTOLOGY

The Norm of Truth

It is important to recall the discussion in Chapter I of the unique form of truth pertinent to religious and theological discussions. Truth in this context, and truth in general when considered as a universal interpretation of the meaning of human existence, is a continuing quest rather than a possession. Rooted in the historicity of human existence, truth can only be affectively experienced and conceptually symbolized in finite symbols, metaphors, and models which attempt to order our human quest and to give meaning and sense to our lives. The quest for universal truth is first and foremost an exercise of our imagination—our ability to image our experiences and to continually check those images in the on-going reality of living in the world. Truth is therefore the experience of a meaningful engagement with life rather than only a copy of external nature or ahistorical essences. If one accepts as axiomatic that human life is most intensely experienced through interpersonal relationships, our quest for truth will be public and common—an exercise of intersubjectivity rather than of objective copying.

Thus we come to the basic questions of the norm of truth for Christology: Do our Christological symbols, metaphors, and models give us an adequate and comprehensive interpretation of the meaning and sense of *our lives together* in the world? Does our Christology adequately address the basic, perennial questions of personal and social living—questions of the meaning of human history itself—as they emerge in our *contemporary* world?

The Norms of Right and Good

Since truth is a lived experience—embedded in practice—our quests for truthful meaning and sense will always confront the moral norms of the right and the good. Since our quests for truth are always intersubjective and social, others are involved and affected. The norm that truth promotes the right and the good involves a critique of the implications of our truth claims for our practical lives in the world—how we are transformed by them, how they transform our society or would transform it if adopted. Finally, the moral norms of right and good extend this notion of personal and social transformation in a specific first direction. And thus, considering the clear New Testament and "Old" Testament prophetic bias for the least advantaged (extended here to include those who are different), the question arises for Christians to consider: How do our Christological claims morally impinge on those outside of our faith experience and conviction? We must therefore ask ourselves if we have *sustained* the basic morality of our truth claims about Jesus the Christ. If not, why not? Can other Christological models be reconstructed that are more truthful because they are more moral?

The Norm of Fidelity

If we are called to be both truthful and moral in our Christological claims, the norm of fidelity requires constant attention. We cannot assume that we are being faithful simply because we rather automatically repeat past Christological formulations. Rather, fidelity requires being faithful to *truthful experiences*—to *interpersonal encounters* that lead to right and good for ourselves and for those with whom we live, or at the very least do them no harm, that affirm rather than negate them, that respect them as free and equal searchers for meaning and life. With this understanding of fidelity, *orthodoxy* is first checked under norms of "ortho-fidelity" (right and true faith) and "ortho-praxis"[1] (right and true action). The norm of fidelity thus asks whether our Christology stimulates and enhances the experience of loving and respectful encounter with both God and neighbor mediated by the one whom we confess to be the Christ, the Son of the living God.

INITIAL THEOLOGICAL NOTES

Personal/Interpersonal Imagery

At the outset, it is important to recall that fundamentally all of our theistic imagery must be either personal or set within a context that intends to disclose personal and interpersonal presence. Personal symbols, metaphors, and stories are not optional in Christian theology; they are demanded by the faith that emerges from what we take to be interpersonal encounters with the *Person* of God.[2]

Christianity's Norm of Monotheism

Christianity is a monotheistic religion and must remain so, avoiding all theological lapses into bi-theism or tri-theism. Classical "orthodox" Christology had every *intention* of avoiding any blatant bi-theism or tri-theism but, as we have seen, its rather tortured philosophical constructions did not capture the simplicity of a faith confession in the one God. And it seems clear that popular Christian faith and theology, formed under the burden of a culturally specified and ancient philosophical system, did not always avoid such dangers. Even though this popular facade of bi-theism and tri-theism has been a constant scandal to Judaism, this is not the main reason why Christology must avoid these lapses. Christianity must remain monotheistic because the faith of Jesus himself was first and last a radically monotheistic one.[3]

Despite the rather non-controversial nature of a Christian theological norm of monotheisim, a question remains. Do the New Testament confessions and incipient theological explanations share, in places, at least the bi-theistic tendency of classical "orthodox" Christologies?[4] I can only raise the question here and recall some of our earlier discussions. Taken as a whole, it seems clear that the New Testament stories are basically about Jesus' relationship with God and the implications that such radical fidelity has for our own self-understanding and salvation. The basic confession of Jesus' faith and intimacy with the one God is now normative for us and paradigmatic for Christian faith. It is, in short, our Christian revelation.

On the other hand, the basic theological and philosophical models used to begin explaining Jesus' radically monotheistic faith (the exercise of the New Testament writers' theological imaginations) are *not* part of our *normative revelation*, but rather of our *theological tradition*. If this part of our biblical heritage lapses at times (or seems to) into a *functional bi-theism*, then it is incumbent upon us both to try to understand why the New Testament authors wrote in these ways (*interpretation*) and to engage the perennial task of critical theological reconstruction (*critique*).

The Trinitarian Paradigm

Even though Christianity must remain monotheistic, it must also retain a basic Trinitarian model and paradigm for imaging God's relation with the world and the world's relation to God (as well as our interrelations with each other). The centering nexus for this tri-partite interrelational paradigm will be the mutual manifestation and revelation of God and world in Jesus, the Christ. My suggestion for reconstructing such a Trinitarian paradigm is to use a basic model of conversant speech—three ways of talking about and imagining God's interrelationship with the world.

God spoken of as creator and source will use the personal metaphors of father and mother.[5] God spoken of as historically involved in the life of one human being who responded to God's invitation in a radically faithful way—a way that is now normatively paradigmatic for Christians, the Christic metaphor for every man and woman—will be spoken of in the Christological titles of Jesus as the Christ, the "Son" (and now, perhaps, "offspring") of God, the Lord.[6] God's continuing presence in the world will be spoken of as the spirit of self-identity and understanding, the spirit of truth and righteousness, the hope of salvation. For Christians, this spirit of God will be incarnated (made present in flesh) in its most intense form through the celebration of the memory of Jesus Christ and in action and work motivated by that celebrated memorial presence.[7]

Despite any similarity with what was historically judged heterodox "modalism,"[8] such a conversational paradigm for Trinitarian theology retains the force of the basic Christian confession of three interpersonal metaphors (a tri-partite symbol) of God's involvement with the world while avoiding the dangers of tritheism. Regardless of the disclaimers of classical Trinitarian theology, its metaphysical modality of *three* persons *in one* presented then and continues to present more of a logical conundrum than a mystery of belief. To *continue* to speak in faith and hope of God as creator and source, of God's intimate involvement with a human being (and with all human beings), of God's continuing presence as both the spirit in and the spirit of the world is mystery enough. Christians continue to speak such words; along with other theistic believers, Christians proclaim that despite any evidence to the contrary, we are all both touched and encompassed by the mystery of God's continuing presence in and for the world. This *is* the faith event.

The Centrality of Jesus, the Christ

This final theological note serves only to highlight what was said above. The central memory for Christians, the basic form for the celebration of God's presence in the world and the world's presence to God, the fundamental motivating force for moral action, is the memory of Jesus the Christ. The Christ is the sacramental nexus—the point of connecting contact embodied in the human experience of Jesus of Nazareth—for the mediation of God and world. Christians celebrate in word, liturgical sacrament, and moral action this sacramental theology—their fundamental and defining belief that in all matters of life and death Jesus Christ is ultimately decisive,[9]—the same Jesus of Nazareth who *is* the Christ, the Son of the living God.

CONSTRUCTIVE FOUNDATIONAL NOTES

Review of the Basic Christian Paradigm

Before we take up a constructive discussion of the basic philosophical and theological terms and models for an adequately reconstructed Christology, it is necessary to review the elements of the Christian paradigm of faith and theology. For this and the following section I will retain the form of an outline of notes which, taken as a whole, intend to set the contours of the fundamental Christic core of Christian faith, the foundations of its self-defining Christology, and the primary motivation for Christian moral action.

(A) The basic question of theistic religion is the relationship between God and world.

GOD
|
WORLD

(B) The basic answer of Christianity—the fundamental and foundational faith—is that God and world are primarily interrelated in Jesus, the Christ.

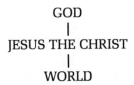

GOD
|
JESUS THE CHRIST
|
WORLD

(C) It is this relationship between God and Jesus—the faith and moral life of Jesus himself—that led the original disciples to confess and proclaim him to be the Christ. It is this confession of faith—their primary interpretation of Jesus as the *world's way to God* and *God's way to the world*—that led them in their "Easter conversion"[10] to the foundational Christian confession.

(D) There are a number of important "truths" of the Christian religion disclosed in this paradigm.

1. Christianity involves a human-personal paradigm for religion.

2. Christianity's basic paradigm and model is interrelational and sacramental—the embodied presentation, communication, and disclosure of God to world and world to God.

3. It is in this interrelational and sacramental context of radical faith that practical moral actions are determined.

4. The quality of Jesus' faith was radically monotheistic.[11]

5. Radical monotheism—the nature of Jesus' relationship with God—is the basic context for interpreting the religious and moral life of Jesus.

6. It is in this radical faith and moral life that Jesus *becomes the Christ* for Christians—his basic interrelational union with God and world.

7. This radical interrelationship of the man Jesus with God and world implies a critique of the human—both an affirmation and a negation of any particular state of the world and culture, a critique of all that is not God.[12]

8. This paradigm of Jesus as the Christ presents a basic tension and paradox at the core of Christianity itself. This paradoxical tension between God and world—the world's affirmation and negation—is resolved only in principle in the life and work of Jesus Christ as the proclamation of reunion and salvation; it emerges perennially as Christians attempt to interrelate Christ and their lives in culture under the critique of radically monotheistic faith.[13]

9. Efforts at proclaiming, communicating, and acting in light of this salvific message—efforts at reconstituting a critical reunion of the spirit of God with and as the spirit of the world, the resolution of the paradox of affirmation and negation, divinity and humanity—have occupied Christian theology and ethics from its beginning.

10. The foundation of these efforts is the belief that the spirit of God in and of the world is made present—reincarnated again and again—in the celebration in word, sacrament, and action of the memory of Jesus the Christ.

Basic Christological Phrases and Models

Jesus' Union with God

To speak of Jesus' union with God is to speak within a paradigm of grace and love—a paradigm of intimate and ultimate interpersonal involvement of divinity and humanity, of God and world. Thus, it is not necessary to speak of a unity of being in a mystical or quasi-mystical sense as a single metaphysical "entity"—expressed in Latin as *ens,* the *noun* for "*a* being." We might very well, however, consider this union as a mergence of being under the metaphors of spiritual and loving intimacy—under a notion of "being" that is actively and verbally constituted, in Latin *esse,* "to be."[14] We commonly and poetically speak of two living partners as having become "one flesh," symbolized and celebrated in their sexual union. Such metaphors of sexual love are not uncommon in biblical usage, especially in the Jewish Bible and the Christian Old Testament.[15] The fact that we *must* speak of the union of God and Jesus in rather indirect, metaphorical and even poetic terms rather than under the guise of some "metaphysical description" is, as we have discussed, neither a reduction of Christian faith nor unusual. It is in fact necessary and certainly more of an inducement to the passionate and relevant enhancement of that faith than is the call for a rather secular "belief" in a particular metaphysical system. The metaphors of living partnership and intimate union certainly seem to be more personally engaging and transforming than appeals to archaic Christological terms such as *homoousion.*

Jesus' Identification with God

Under a paradigm of union in grace and love, Jesus is not to be identified with God as one and the same "being." Even classical Christology attempted to retain some distinction among the persons of the Trinity. However, the notion of an identification in being remained. If we are to keep alive a sense of the interrelationship between God and Jesus—the basic Christic paradigm of Jesus' radically monotheistic fidelity—then we must keep the note of *distinction without separation* constant in our Christological formulations: the active mergence of "beings" in their "being." The reason that Christians confess Jesus to be the Christ is because of his intimate *union* with God and the proclamation, revelation, and promise that such a union of grace and love is offered to human beings as well. And so, we attempt to reconstruct a Christology that highlights the interrelational distinction of Jesus and God while proclaiming, as part of our Easter faith, that their intimate union conquered all attempts at separation—even death. In the Christological paradigm of the interrelationship between

Jesus and God we cannot without dilution speak of Jesus' identification with God; we must rather speak of a divine-human union that is salvific and normative—the union of God and world, of spirit and flesh, indeed of persons and persons.

Jesus' Equality with God

The question of Jesus' equality with God returns us again to our discussion of the New Testament and conciliar Christological models noted in Chapter III. Here I will divide the basic models into ontological/cosmological and moral/practical ones. The concept of the equality of God and Jesus is a difficult one, but it remains a foundational metaphor for Christian faith and theology. In short, I think that it is necessary (without a simple identification of Jesus and God) to speak of some kind of equality.

Ontological/Cosmological Models

Ontological models—those that emphasize Jesus' equality in being with God—exhibit many of the same problems that we have discussed with attempts to denote an identification of being. If in fact we wish—as I think we must—to maintain the note of the interrelationship of Jesus with God, then to speak of ontological equality tends to dissolve the religious and moral tension involved in the phenomenon of radical fidelity; such fidelity is indicated in the New Testament as Jesus' radical commitment to doing the "Father's" will. At the same time the paradigm of Jesus Christ as the center of the divine-human encounter is similarly reduced to an encounter between "gods." The life of Jesus as one of human struggle for fidelity in faith and action tends to be viewed (at least in popular faith) as a dramatic charade of total control— a life totally planned, a future entirely known.

Cosmological Christological models which emphasize an equality in status and role in the cosmos or an equality of power over the universe exhibit similar problems. The pre-existent Word of God "descending" to earth, incarnated as Jesus of Nazareth, living, dying, rising and "ascending" again to a place of triumphant regency over the universe, presents very real problems for maintaining the theological note of the humanity of Jesus as the Christ.

Even though we may understand the attraction of such cosmological imaginings during the New Testament era,[16] we must ask if these "triumphal" metaphors are still viable as the core of a contemporary Christology. We no longer utilize the ancient cosmologies to explain the scientific workings of the universe; in both its assets and liabilities, the scientific revolution has challenged these classical Christological formulations. In its challenge to traditional cosmological formulations, the scientific revolution has in fact stimulated Christian theology to recover the basic force and power of religious metaphorical speech. What we can no longer say in descriptive cosmological terms can now be recovered again in speech that moves to the depths of the human heart and spirit. Religion is finally not about the physical makeup of the universe. Rather, it is about the meaning of our human experiences—the sense and meaning of human history and our own self-identification and understanding as human beings in the world. If science forces theistic religion to turn inward and earthward to personal and interpersonal metaphors for disclosing our normative relation with God and with each other, it will have performed a great service. If it challenges Christianity to see the mystery of Jesus the Christ as one of grace and love, one of radical intimacy and passionate commitment with and to God and world, then our attention will have been directed to its proper earthly and actional locus.

By discriminating the roles and functions of science and religion we can discover that both are necessary for advancing the human search for understanding, knowledge, and meaning. Religion can thus end its classic debate with science and get on with the task of recovering experiences of transcendence so often lost when science and technology are given the field as a comprehensive interpretation of the meaning of human existence. Cosmological Christologies simply no longer function as they did in the New Testament era. Nonetheless, by the adoption of more "earthbound" models and metaphors the intention of such Christologies can be maintained and re-presented in ways that enhance the Christian faith. I will discuss one such attempt in the final section of this chapter. However, a further note is necessary.

We have already discussed the dangers for non-Christians of an overly triumphal Christology, especially when it is carried over into a triumphal notion of the Church and ecclesial function-

ing. The marriage of triumphant Christianity and political power
has not been a happy one both for the Church and for those outside of it. Again, at least the legitimate intention of triumphant
Christianity to celebrate God's victory over sin and death can be
maintained to some extent even in more earth-bound Christological models and metaphors—the belief that Jesus conquered infidelity and banality, hatred and sin, death itself. Power over the
forces of nature is not the only way to speak of such triumphs, nor
is it finally the most appropriate way to express the victory of
good over evil as the essence of human salvation. The force of
successful interpersonal living—lives of peace, justice, and love—
is by far the more promising reservoir for models and metaphors
of such salvation.

However, we should not jump too quickly or too optimistical-
ly to even this more promising resource for Christological models.
If the challenge of the scientific resolution can result in hope for a
renewal of religious and theistic language, it also presents a dark-
er challenge to the continuing relevance of all types of salvational
speech in general—challenging the power of any interpersonal
and interhuman relationship to finally achieve the victory of good
over human evil in its most radical form. Perhaps for the first time
in human history, it seems that scientific technology has presented the proximate possibility of the victory of radical evil over
good. The promethean power and diabolic prospect of nuclear an-
nihilation thus presents a challenge heretofore unknown for theistic religion. In the face of the possibility of a nuclear holocaust,
for theistic religion and, particularly, for Christianity to continue
to speak (in what often seems like facile homiletic terms) of the
ultimate, almighty power of God (or God in Jesus) to control the
cosmos and effect the final victory of good over evil borders on
presumption and naiveté. And whatever one might say of the su-
prarational nature of commitments of faith and love, neither
ought to be presumptive or naive. It often seems that we speak
too easily of God's almighty power over the cosmos. Could it be
that this dark side of the scientific revolution has finally put to a
debilitating test all such false and presumptive hope? In light of
this, it seems more theologically correct for believers to confess
that God's creation of free human subjects was in fact *a relin-
quishment of such power.* We must therefore go on to explain that

this creaturely freedom can obviously be used for good or abused for evil.

As history shows the capacity for evil seems to radically intensify in direct correlation to our advancing scientific abilities to destroy, maim and kill. Our own deadly century surely challenges us to overcome this dangerous theological naiveté. Even with such caution at facile confessions of God's almighty power and false hopes for the ultimate triumph of good over evil in some pre-determined evolutionary sense—for Christians, the final cosmological victory of the "second coming"—we are not left without real albeit chastened hope. We can in fact be encouraged in the knowledge that despite our own rather evident failures, the spirit of God remains alive in the world, waiting to be recalled and made present again as we work together with faith to accomplish God's intentions for creation. In a paradoxical way we, who have been *saved by God*, and for Christians, in Christ, must now become *saviors of God* and God's creation.[17]

Moral/Practical Models

If there are difficulties in speaking of Jesus' equality with God in cosmological terms, there may be more promise of speaking of it in moral-practical ways, though even here we will not be problem-free. Surely it is not difficult for Christians (and possibly non-Christians as well) to speak affirmatively of Jesus' moral intentions—the intentions of a good and holy man to bring his will and purpose (and, for Christians, his being) into conformity with God's: advancing the welfare and well-being of creation. Such an intentional hope for the triumph of goodness and right was not without its frustrations and suffering for both Jesus and, in light of the above, for God. In any empirically objective sense, Jesus' hope has not been realized. If Christian belief is to speak accurately of his victory and triumph, it will do so in terms that indicate that despite all evidence to the contrary, the hope remains alive—the hope that motivates action and work. Thus, Christian faith can indeed confess that Jesus achieved an equality with God in his hope for the world as well as in his sorrow over the world.

If we wish to continue with this moral/practical Christologi-

cal model and speak of an equality of "character" of Jesus and
God, more caution must be taken. As a rule, in Christian theology
God is the perfection of virtue by definition. If we cast Jesus according to this basically essentialist notion—Jesus as an expression of the essence of all virtues—we return to the same problem
of maintaining a full understanding of Jesus' humanity and in that
the problem of retaining the full power of our paradigmatic model
of a *divine-human* interrelationship. I have argued that all of our
God-language is naturally indirect, symbolic, metaphorical, and
analogical. Our language about Jesus has often been of the same
variety; *it need not always be so.* The historical human experience of Jesus of Nazareth, even if only tangentially described in
the New Testament, gives us a referent for our human imagination that we simply do not have when we attempt to talk of God.
We ourselves have direct experience of what it means to be human in the world—the basic paradoxes of goodness and evil, virtue and vice. To cast the character of Jesus in the same analogical
way in which we cast the "character" of God diminishes the opportunity for our moral and theological imaginations to relate in
faith to the struggles of Jesus' own quest for radical faith and
commitment. If we therefore ask: "Was Jesus the perfect human
being?" "Was he equal in moral perfection with God?" our answers seem to be contained in the way in which we use our moral
and theological imaginations. If we concentrate on what I have
described as the basic Christological paradigm of Jesus as the mediation of God and world, then we must of necessity include both
forms of speech concerning the "character" of God and the "character" of the human condition. In this sense we can say that Jesus
mediated for us the perfection of God but, at the same time, the
revelation of the paradoxical nature of the human condition. In
the titles of "the Christ," "the Son of the living God," and "the
Lord," Jesus presents both God's perfection—the fullness of truth
and right—as well as the paradoxical struggle of every man and
woman with good and evil. To speak of Jesus as the perfect human being does not do justice to the basic Christic paradigm of
the Christian faith. Therefore, Jesus must represent for us not only
divine perfection but also human imperfection, temptation, and
sin.[18] At the same time, Christian faith confesses that despite the
tensions, struggles, and sins of human existence, Jesus was finally

faithful. Such a confession proclaims Jesus' own triumph and the Christian hope.

A CONSTRUCTIVE SUGGESTION: A DIALOGIC CHRISTOLOGY

I will conclude these notes for a reconstructed non-negating Christology with a direction toward the *metaphor of dialogue* for a *new Christological model.* A dialogic Christological model focuses our theological imagination on a common, everyday human activity. It seems to me, as I have argued, that if theological models are to remain relevant, if they are to continue to enhance the faith amid all the changes in the canons of meaning and knowledge as we move through history, then the more commonly universal the metaphors and models used, the better. That deep interpersonal encounters stimulated and effected by the interactive word may now be under assault in our own cybernetic society only increases the attractiveness of this metaphor and model in light of the fullness of our biblical heritage.

Full dialogue involves a reciprocity of listening and speaking, of contemplation and action, by at least two distinct partners who are brought together in the intimacy of the dialogic exchange. Dialogic partners are always distinct from each other while at the same time not separate, always co-present with each other as long as the dialogue continues. The dialogic union effected by the word can be as intimate as the depth of the dialogue itself. The understanding achieved by the partners in any dialogic exchange involves a mergence or fusion of their own particular perspectives, a fusion of their own dialogically interacting beings, and a mergence of thoughts, intentions and wills. Each person retains a separate identity, yet with the prospect and hope for union. While the exchange does not need to be totally symmetrical (even at its initial starting point), the freedom of the dialogue itself creates a situation of equality between (or among) the partners. Thus we can speak of a particular kind of "dialogic equality" of the partners.

Once we cast the basic elements of our Christological notes
onto the framework of a dialogic model, we can discover a way to
interrelate the notions of identification, union, and equality involved in the basic dialogic interrelationship between God and
Jesus. God and Jesus retain the necessary "individuation" of
speaking partners. Their interpersonal union of grace, love, intention, will, and action are effected in the depths of their dialogic
exchange. Jesus attains a mergence and fusion with God, an
equality with God, in the process of their deep and faithful dialogic exchange. One can even speak of this equality as one of being,
if by that is meant a union effected by the spoken word—the
word (and words) that are in fact fundamental actuations of our
being-in-the-world. We express ourselves most fundamentally
and offer our personal beings as actors in the world to others *first
and foremost* through the dialogic word.[19] Words connect; they
unify; they effect interpersonal unions with selves in the world.
Words also disconnect, break apart interpersonal unions, effect
splits of hatred and death. What Christian faith claims that Jesus
accomplished in his dialogic union with God—his *dialogic* equality—could have in fact failed. Words are ambiguous. Christian
faith confesses that Jesus immersed himself in that ambiguity and
offers to us a life that was triumphant because of the dialogic
union it accomplished between divinity and humanity.

As the center of the divine-human dialogue, Christians can
continue to confess that Jesus is *God's word for us,* and *our word
for God.*[20] The Spirit of that paradigmatic divine-human dialogue
remains alive in faith and action where these "words" are remem-
bered, celebrated, and incarnated again when human persons and
human institutions continue to effect just, peaceful, and even, at
times, intimate interrelationships.

My initial outline for a dialogic Christological model needs finally to be subjected to the criteria of adequacy suggested earlier.
It is an exercise in theological imagination that intends to suggest
a Christological model that *can be* true, moral, and faithful. The
prospects for its truth can be ascertained by attention to the universal and fundamental quality of the phenomenon of dialogue itself. If, as I have argued, it is through dialogic speech that we
gather our basic sense and meaning of being human in the world,
make our initial and most intimate contacts with others, express
and actuate ourselves as personal *beings* (as interactive "verbs"),

then the metaphor of dialogue and the Christological model it grounds can indeed present a comprehensive framework for our own continuing quest for truth. The truth of the faith in the divine-human dialogue between God and Jesus is thus determined in what it says to us about our own efforts at self-understanding as we intersubjectively and socially move through history with a vision of what a just, peaceful and loving historical existence ought to be.

Truth, as always, thus turns eventually on our own quests for the right and the good. A dialogic society would be one where each person is respected as an equal partner. Freedom, equality and mutual respect would be assured. No one person or group would be negated as unworthy of participation in the dialogic exchange. Those with the most difficulty in making their voice heard—the least advantaged—would be given first priority. Actions would be results of mutual dialogic understandings and judgments, rather than the monologues of dogmatic authoritarianism or totalitarian power and terror. Mistakes, even sins, would not be ruled out, but the foundational norms of on-going dialogue would make the prospect of correction and conversion more likely. If a dialogic Christological model gives theological grounds for pursuing such a norm for interpersonal and societal interaction, then its prospects for being adequately moral are enhanced as well.

Finally, a dialogical Christological model must be subjected to the norm of fidelity. Under our constructive norm, does such a Christology enhance the faith, make our tradition more understandable, make us more faithful to our own origins and to those who do not share these origins? It is important to note again the simple theological axiom that the more humanly universal our theological metaphors and models, the more chance they have of enhancing our faith as meaningful. My contention is that dialogue is just such a universal human experience—a foundational one that discloses to us how in fact we are in the world and how in fact we ought to be when we either forget or deny these foundations of human being and existence. Thus, the Christological model of dialogue stands as a reminder of what fidelity means—what it means to be faithful to God, to ourselves, and to each other symbolized and made present for us in the remembrance and celebration of Jesus as the Christ. At the same time, despite some discontinuity with the dogmatic and doctrinal formulations of traditional Christological orthodoxy—and there are some in this model, as I have indicated—the basic essence of the faith is, I believe, intact.

In the dialogic Christological model, God remains monotheistic without philosophical gymnastics or theological sleights of hand. Jesus remains, as he must for Christian faith, fully human. God and Jesus are joined in a union of such intimacy that we may speak of their dialogic equality and even of their union in being. Our basic Trinitarian model of God's original creative word, God's word to and for us in Jesus, and God's continuing word in the reincarnation of the Spirit of the divine-human Christological encounter retains its traditional force in Christian faith and life. Finally, the dialogic union accomplished in Jesus' radical fidelity to God—the graced union of divinity and humanity, God and world—remains both a possibility and a promise for us. We have only to enter in and take part in faith and action in their dialogic exchange—an exchange that finally must include all of the human family, each member equally respected and listened to as they speak their own words of peace and life.

Appendix
"I AM THE WAY, THE TRUTH AND THE LIFE": THE EXCLUSIVITY AND SINGULARITY OF CHRISTIAN CLAIMS

INTRODUCTION

In Chapter I I emphasized the qualities of uniqueness and plurality which surround religious claims in general and monotheistic and Christian claims in particular. In a note to that chapter, I indicated that more needed to be said about a third quality of monotheistic claims: exclusive singularity. Throughout, I have indicated how such claims for religious and theistic truth might emerge, and the place in which to locate them has at least been suggested. This seemed all that was appropriate for the basic text of an essay that intends to advance a more realistic foundation for Christian-Jewish dialogue. However, if such dialogue is not to be pre-programmed to either facile resolution or rather "weak" expressions of the right to differ, the issues of exclusive and singular claims to truth must be addressed. Real ecumenical dialogue will eventually have to address each participant at the level of their strongest claims and most forceful self-understanding and confession. I have, therefore, chosen to advance our inquiry into the strongest possible religious claims that monotheists in general, and Christians and Jews in particular, are enjoined to make—their claims for exclusive and singular truth—by way of an Appendix. It will be evident that our inquiry, though preliminary, will move at levels of greater abstraction than much of the main body of the text. The issue we are engaging is difficult and close reasoning is called for. Just as in the text, however, this Appendix shares a practical perspective and a moral intent. For we come to this reflection and interpretation from the negative moral history of Christian-Jewish relations with the specific intention of offering some assistance for the alleviation of that historical scandal.

In what follows, therefore, I will discuss further the proper placement and use of the Christian claim for exclusive and singular truth in our confession of Jesus as the *one* way, the *one* truth, and the *one* life—the *only* Christ and Lord of all. At the same time, I will describe how such claims can be and are abused. Even though my basic interest will be to discuss the Christian claim of exclusive singularity, I will draw parallels with monotheism in general, which necessarily includes Judaism. With such a parallel, it becomes clear how Christians *and* Jews are obliged by the self-understandings of their own traditions to confess the one and "no other" God, and Christians, Jesus the one and "no other" Christ and Lord, Son of the living God. However, at the same time that Christians and Jews engage in such self-confessions, they engage the risk of serious abuse through the misuse of their claims with respect to each other and other religious traditions as well.

THE TASK:
GIVING AN ACCOUNT OF CHRISTIAN CLAIMS

Throughout the text, and especially in Chapters I and IV, I noted the rather "hypothetical" character of the meaning, meaningfulness, and truth[1] of religious, theistic and Christian claims. Since I suggested that events of religious faith take priority over theological claims, I argued that the emergence of the claims for truth and right which frame monotheistic language finally make sense only *if* and *after* the event of an encounter of religious presence—only after the grasp of faith and the draw of love.[2] However, once we posit this event of encounter—the experience of presence that defines the very nature of religious reality—our task is then to describe and properly locate the language and the claims that we use to confess and talk about what we have experienced and, indeed, about what has happened to us. This, therefore, was the context for our earlier discussions of the uniqueness and plurality of religious and theistic language and claims. We recognized that our religious experience of theistic encounter— our experience of divine-human presence—will be unique (as special) for us. We also recognized that there are in fact a plurality of such special encounters among the many religious experiences in the world (for example, the "encounters" of both Christians and Jews as well as among Christians and Jews). At the same time, we recognize that our respective claims for what has happened to us will have universal implications for how we are in the world in terms of everyone and everything else.

Therefore, language and claims that must in fact begin only after a uniquely gracious event of encountered presence (the religious/theistic experience) move immediately to the level of universal implication despite the evident plurality of such intensely personal happenings.[3] What is so intensely special to me, to us, or to any number of others in plural and different ways always has implications for all others as well—and, so we tend to claim, especially for those who have not encountered religious presence in just our way. Thus, despite the uniqueness and plurality of Christian and Jewish claims, our confessions of faith and truth pertain also to all others. It is indeed the paradox of at least monotheistic religions (if not religion in general) that what happens to us as a unique grace—multiple and plural encounters of sacred and, for theists, personal presence—must by nature of the event assume a status of universal relevance and applicability. For monotheists, this universality of experience and language confession—the encounter with the one God of all—eventually leads to claims of exclusive singularity.

To summarize: I am suggesting that the montheistic religious experience will necessarily be cast as a universal one that expresses notes in its confession and telling of not only uniqueness and plurality, but also of singularity. What we experience is not our own special truth "just for us" among which there are many others, but *the one truth*—the one and only God of and for all, the one and only Christ, Lord and Savior of and for all. In its nature, monotheism in general and Christian monotheism in particular must include this note of singularity.

It is of the utmost importance, however, to understand that our claims for exclusivity and singularity are not of the logical variety. As I have argued in the text, since in religious experience and confession we are not operating in linguistic and epistemological worlds of simple "descriptive" language or hard and fast "logical rules," we should not and, indeed, cannot advance religious claims of *logical* exclusivity or singularity. It is, therefore, never accurate to advance any religious claim on the basis that "if this is so" (our event of divine-human encounter) "that is not so" (the event of divine-human encounter of another). As I have noted throughout, we must locate religious, theistic, and Christian languages and their attendant claims in the milieu of experiential and "eventing" meaning, meaningfulness and truth—in the milieu of presence and encounter, *not* in the milieu of logical description. Our task of giving an account of Christian claims for singularity, then, will never be adequately accomplished if engaged as a question of logical truth or error. The meaning and truth we seek can only be verified in the milieu of experiences of encountered presence.

Recall that with the task of verifying truth goes the necessity of its legitimation. Legitimation—the maintenance of the truth of our claims in their promotion of the right and good—can only come about by critically interpreting, gauging, and judging their effects in the world, the truth in practice. This movement between verification and legitimation constitutes the praxis of the critical tradition of religious and theistic claims; it also constitutes our ongoing challenge of maintaining the truth that we confess.

Claims for Singularity: Stage One

Even though we know that there are a plurality of claims for the divine-human encounter (claims of religious and theistic presence), in their uniqueness such claims are not transferrable. To speak of a logical transfer of "true" love from this person to that involves a statistical abstraction and makes little substantive and concrete sense. Neither, then, does it make sense to discuss a logical transfer of religious experiences before personally existential encounters of new presence which might effect a conversion. It thus seems that in those deep encounters of religious presence, we find the single, exclusive way of being in the world *for us.* In naming our encounter as a presence with the one God and the one Christ, we confess for *ourselves* the single way of truth and life. Christianity, therefore, becomes for *us* the universal way that *we* are in the world with others. It is the way that we make sense of others—come to meaning, meaningfulness, truth and right with them. Our exclusive and singular Christian confession is also *for* them in this sense: if they are to be with us and we with them, they are asked to interpret, understand, and act with us in terms of this self and collective identity. In short, *this* is who *we* are.

Claims for Singularity: Stage Two

With this note of self and collective identity, we move to the next step in accounting for our Christian claims of singular truth. Christians in fact make claims that the God in Christ whom they encounter is the God and the Christ of and for all—the Creator and Sustainer of the universe, the Lord and Redeemer. Christians, however, ought to make this claim carefully without trying to force others to name what appears to them in just the same way—namely, God in Christ as an invitation to presence. As I have indicated, such "forcing" by "logical" demonstration or manipulation toward "conversion" is based on a radical misunderstanding of the nature of such encounters of presence—the basic character of faith and love as interpersonal events.

Christians make such claims, then, because of their most basic religious experience itself, an experience whose notes of exclusivity and singularity are part of the generic phenomenon of monotheism. The Christian monotheistic experience is an act of sacramentally naming what/who appears to us as an encounter in presence with the one God in the one Christ.

In other words, embedded in the very nature of the Christian monotheistic experience—as in monotheism in general—is the claim that "there can be no other." In this light, it is most important to understand that *the claim of singularity is not a later logical deduction or theological addition.* In the first instance it is intrinsic in the phenomenon of the monotheistic and Christian monotheistic encounter of presence.

The claim of full singularity, then, is part of our own self and collective experience of identity. It is part of our confession, our narrative history, and human/Christian character; it is the auto-biographical story that we tell; it is our very individual and collective selves; it is who we are, our own name. Thus, the God in Christ whom we have named as the "Other" of our encounter becomes part and, indeed, the ground of our own name as a people. Just as I am who I am as an individual only because of those whom I have encountered as my biographical heritage—my own tradition of coming to be—there is no other possible me. I am my own name.

To imagine another *like* me is possible as analogy. However, to logically posit another possible me would only be an abstraction with no concrete historical content. Even if such a logical exercise were possible, it would have no relevance for understanding religious experience, since the nature of that experience is rooted not in the logical "idea" but in the phenomenological encounter. Again, religious experience is framed existentially and phenomenologically—in the grasp of faith and the draw of love. Therefore, *religious experience,* not logical idea, is the proper *foundational context* for interpreting and evaluating confessional claims as well as for grounding all later theological construction.

Existentially and phenomenologically, then, there can be no other me. If my own name is finally merged with the name of the Other who confronts me (in the sense that now I do not only *believe in* the doctrine of Christian monotheism, but *am* in fact a Christian monotheist), then my claim for myself and the Other at this level can only be a singular one. There can be no other me and there can be no other Other in whom I become who I am.[4]

If the above account of the phenomenon of religious experience is so, and if, in light of that experience, my location and interpretation of the status of monotheistic and Christian claims is accurate, then we can again see that our claims for singularity do not attain sense and meaning at the level of ordinary logical description. At the same time, the Christian monotheistic confession of the Christ as the "one way," the "one truth," and the "one life" cannot attain the prospect of being judged meaningful, true, and right at any level other than that of biographical confession and praxis. The persuasive quality of such biographical claims are never finally of a logical variety which highlights the force of argument. In the best sense of the term, argument does have a place in systematic theological conversation. However, its proper place is not its use as a "demonstration" of the validity of our primary claims of singular Christian truth—demonstrations that others could and would accept if only they were not so blind or had not perversely chosen not to see.

Once we begin to understand this difference between the phenomenological and logical levels of human experience, we can more easily understand what in fact full conversion (from one truth to another) means. Such conversion involves a change in self and collective identity—beginning to tell a new story about ourselves; becoming, as it were, someone different. Obviously, such "full conversions" are rare; they transcend logical argument; they can never be forced. In one way or another, all religious experience transcends ordinary logical realms of everyday life. At this first transcending level, the uniqueness and plurality of religious experiences ought to be fairly evident and to a great extent liberally accepted. However, monotheistic experience moves us to a second transcending level, including but moving a step beyond the notes of uniqueness and plurality. It is here that the confusion of the phenomenological and logical becomes so common and so critical. Again, we must return to the existential hypothesis of the grasp of faith and the draw of love. Only *if* and *after* we experience the phenomenon of an encounter of Christian monotheistic presence can our claims of one way, truth, and life have any validity whatsoever or any real prospect of being legitimated as right. At least since the dawning of the modern Enlightenment, the Christian problem has been to understand how we can be liberally accepting of other religious claims while passionately confessing our own as the "one way," not only for us but for "them" as well. In this Appendix I am presenting an entree to this problem which attempts on the one hand to take seriously the requirements of a monotheistic confession, while on the other to call for necessary human and Christian obligations of affirmation and respect—obligations drawn most especially and primarily toward those whose names are most strange to us.

Therefore, I have argued that only at the phenomenal level of encounter in presence—at the level of what I take to be the nature of true religion—can we begin to see how such claims are part of our self and collective understanding. Claims of singularity are thus not optional for the monotheistic Christian but are in fact necessary if we are to be who we are and if others are to be with us and know us by name. For a Christian to confess Jesus as "the way, the truth and the life" means that we have found this to be our understanding of what being a human in the world finally means. That we must say this of ourselves because we have been "grasped" and "drawn" in a certain way ought not to mean that we need to negate or coerce any *other*. On the contrary, such a confession of phenomenological identification—*our* own speaking of *our* distinctive name—gives us the ground for accepting and respecting the religious names of others. We properly and legitimately make claims of exclusivity and singularity only when we come to understand the one ground on which *our* self-identity rests. We do not and cannot expect others to share that name but must grant them initial respect for who they are. We ought not to be threatened by them nor they by us if our own single ground of self-understanding is secure. Peter's confession in response to Jesus' question of identification—"Who do you say that I am?"—is at the same time our Christian self-identification. This question and Peter's response of naming has set the foundational phenomenological theme of this work. Finally, it is the phenomenal event of presence that gives us our single Christian name and directs us toward understanding, affirmation and respect of others who have uniquely confessed a plurality of other religious/human names. Christians, like all monotheists, make claims of singularity not to imply logical exclusivity but rather phenomenological identity.

SUMMARY

Levels of Christian Claims

In summary, we can distinguish a variety of levels with respect to the question of the nature and status of Christian claims. At one level a claim is *either* true *or* not; it cannot be both. This is

the ordinary level of descriptive fact governed by ordinary canons of logical non-contradiction; that is, a truth claim ordinarily
and logically excludes its counter-claim. If one deals with the
question of the truth of Christianity at this level, then the issue is
posed in such a way that one is left with a clear choice: Christianity is *either* true *or* not—Jesus is the way, the truth and the life or
he is not. I have argued that this is the most problematic and inadequate level upon which to engage the question of the status of
religious claims.

At another level we encounter what can be called "both/
and" claims. At this primary phenomenal level of event, a happening can be true in the uniqueness of its presence for us, while
we admit at the same time that there can be a plurality of such
unique encounters with what appears to be truth. This has indeed
happened to me (to us) in such a unique way that the event
is converting and primarily reorienting for understanding my past
and charting my future—it is *for me* the truth. Similar events have
and are happening to others. Thus, there will always be a plurality of these uniquely true events. Because of the unique quality of
these experiences of reorienting presence, there can be no logical
transfer through argument of these experiences among persons
and groups. At this level, truth is both unique and plural; it is not
subject to the canons of ordinary descriptive logic except insofar
as we want to avoid misapprehension and misidentification.
Keeping in mind that the legitimation of such experiences is only
prospective, the question of validation is trans-logical: it can be
engaged adequately only at the level of primary religious meaning—at the level of personal and collective confession.

Finally, we come to the level where I suggest full claims for
the exclusive and singular nature of religious truth can and, indeed, must be made in the monotheistic tradition. Even though
Christian monotheism does claim that "this truth is one, there is
no other," there are stages in the movement to the claim of full
singularity. The task now, as throughout, is to describe the strongest possible claim that Christians are required to make according to the meaning of their monotheism. If after such a
description, we find at the same time that Christians not only are
not required but in fact *cannot* validly and legitimately negate
other religious and theistic traditions, my project will at least be
initially successful. Paradoxically, it is the maximalist statement

of the Christian monotheistic confession that makes this goal achievable, not any minimalist one.[5]

At the level of interpersonal encounter and naming—the confessional level of primary religious meaning and experience—the One whom we experience as present with us appears not only as a unique encounter in our lives, but in the singular, as one person. Part of the experience of *presence* with an "other" is that the person present with us is unique and singular. This is part of the fullness of what it means to be present with another. There is no other person who is *this* person. I am engaged with this person in a unique and singular way—I am present with him or her. To this point, there is a rather easily drawn analogy between the monotheistic presence with God and all other full encounters of interpersonal presence: there is no other one who is *this One.*

However, with the Christian monotheistic tradition there is an important difference. The note of singularity in Christian claims is carried to a deeper level of singular identity. The God whom we claim to experience in Jesus the Christ is not just *the single Other,* but there is in fact no other Christian experience of God *other than in Jesus Christ.* Thus, we have moved from the singularity of the "mere" phenomenon of being present with another, to the claim of being present with the only Other (God), to the claim that this presence in Christ is the only way for Christians to experience the otherness of God. Even though we are now at the level of singular identity for being a Christian and despite the obvious circularity of our claim ("a Christian must be a Christian if a Christian is to be a Christian"), this is still not the full claim that Christians do and must make.

Full Christian monotheism implies more than the claim of a *unique* encounter *for us.* Rather, the God in Christ whom we claim to encounter is confessed as the God of all that is and the Christ of all who are. Thus, in our experience of naming what we have "seen and heard," we are in fact proclaiming a self-in-collective identity. We are *describing, proclaiming, and confessing* how we have been grasped and drawn. Our claim for singularity, therefore, *only* has validity and initial legitimation at this level of naming—the naming of God in Christ, which becomes our naming of ourselves in the world.

Such claims are not exercises of deductive or inductive logic. We do not argue for our own name, nor do we expect others to have our name. We rather speak it as a way of locating our own experience of coming to be in the world—how we have come and are coming to presence. Our claims that "this is the creator God made present in Jesus the Christ" are in fact confessions of self-in-collective identity—who, what, and how we are in the world. We have no other name nor any other religious identity. We are who we are for ourselves and for all others. Only in this sense can we validly claim that the God whom we experience in Jesus is for ourselves and for all others the one God and one Christ of all— the way that we are ourselves and with all others.

We know that others make similar claims, at least in terms of the phenomena of religious, theistic, and monotheistic experiences. We thus know that there is both phenomenal and historical plurality. Yet we (and "they") know that in narrating our own biographical story, in stating and identifying our character as people in the world, we must not only understand our uniqueness and admit to plurality; as monotheists, we claim full singularity as well. In short, a claim such as this is drawn from the nature of monotheistic and Christian monotheistic experience and makes sense (has meaning, meaningfulness, and truth) only as part of what H.R. Niebuhr calls our "internal history."[6] Thus, at this level of self-in-collective identity—at the level of our primary and "world-orienting" encounters of divine-human presence—we admit to no plurality. Again, such a confession is our own single name.

Internal and External History

It will be helpful to continue this summary with a brief discussion of the question in terms of H. Richard Niebuhr's categories of "internal and external history." Simply stated, for Niebuhr "internal history" is the history of ourselves, our confessional stories, our history "as it is lived and apprehended from within."[7] "External history," on the other hand, is history contemplated and, indeed, interpreted "from the outside"[8]—in the terms we have been using, by those not grasped and drawn like us in our primary experiences of religious and theistic presence. In any use of categories such as these, it is important to remember that we are dealing with relatively ideal typologies offered as ordering principles for the sake of clearer thinking. In our experience of "real" history, such discriminations are never quite so neat.

To continue with our typification, however, in some ways we could further conceive of our internal history as what we say of ourselves, both to ourselves and to others. The same could be said of the internal histories of others. What is said of oneself, of course, often leads to actions that affect others—becomes part of their external history—as has been the case in Christian-Jewish relations. Thus, it is true that internal and external histories, as combinations and recombinations of words and actions, always interrelate.

Niebuhr's categories can further illumine our earlier discussion of those various levels used to determine the truth status of Christian claims. At the logical "either/or" level we are at the point of external historical description: "This is what others say of themselves, how *we* hear *them* and have been affected by them, or it is not." Recalling what we noted about ideal typologies, it is important to mention again that there is never any *purely* descriptive and non-interpreted history, even though for our purposes I think there is some sense to the "either/or" quality of this kind of "descriptive observation." We will refer to this level as Level I.

At Level II we can note a mix of internal and external histories under the conditions of dialogue amid a plurality of religious/theistic claims. As our internal history, truth is unique for us, with a recognition that there is a plurality of such unique internal histories (as phenomena) much like our own. As we described above, our internal history becomes our external history when "heard" by others and/or when it affects others; their internal history functions in a similar way with respect to us. In this interchange of perspectives, we can find an understanding which can lead to proper dialogic forms of respectful yet critical interaction amid religious and theistic pluralism. At the very least, the use of the categories of internal and external histories, along with an understanding of their interaction, could allow Christians and Jews to better locate, interpret, and understand their own tragic history. And while understanding alone does not bring change, it is a necessary first step.

Level III encompasses the relatively pure phenomenal experience of that naming encounter which effects the development of internal history. At this level we both express and continually form our own self-in-collective identity, our own story. Here, the dialogic mix of unique and plural qualities of our claims for truth noted at Level II gives way to exclusive and singular claims. At this level of internal history alone, *and at no other*, we find the proper location of our confession: "There is one God in Christ of and for all, there is no other." Plurality has no place at this level of deep self-understanding and identity; here we only confess who, what, and how we are in the world. Speaking from the context of internal history (Level III), we need no longer utilize the important qualification, "for us" of Level II. Likewise, the hypothetical qualification of the previous level—"if we have or claim to have had this sort of divine-human encounter of presence"—is no longer necessary. At Level III we are relating an internal history that *we* are *certain* about; we have named what has happened to us, a happening now definitive of our narrative biography and character-story. Those who wish to know us at the level at which we claim to know ourselves—at a depth that more often than not eludes both us and them—will come to understand how and why we, as all monotheists, finally make exclusive and singular claims for the truth.

Levels of Religious and Theistic Language: Types of Religious and Theological Discourse

In the final summation, it may be helpful to see how religious/theistic language and theology fit if we merge the two schemas as we have outlined above. At Level I, in the "either/or" of external history, we find religion engaged in a relatively "analytic" and "scientific" study. Here we are interested in learning what others claim about themselves and what we claim about ourselves from the perspective of an "objective" observer—the "scientific" analyst. We will want to know how such claims come about and how they stand tests of coherence; we will seek as well as judge the quality of their fit with other aspects of our life experiences. At the same time, we will investigate how religious and theistic claims have affected ourselves and others "externally" in the world. In general at this level we are engaged in basic descriptions, analyses, and expositions of the plurality of religious, theistic and Christian languages and claims. Always remembering the rather ideal nature of these typological levels, at Level I we investigate according to the basic norm that this or that is *either* claimed *or* not, had or has this *or* that effect or not. Work at this level is most often called the "scientific" (or "academic") study of religion.

At Level II the attempt emerges to become constructive and systematic in a theological way. I have already indicated how the qualification "constructive" is here used in theology to indicate both an internal and external interrelationship between critical theological inquiry and faith.[9] Thus, from our own perspective and from the perspective of the other, constructive theology attempts to interrelate faith and life in such a way that sense, meaning, meaningfulness and truth are advanced. At this level, therefore, theology attempts to positively construct basic models and paradigms as meaning systems for interpreting and understanding the world and our place in it. Our theological dialogue at Level II will respect and engage a plurality of perspectives, all with a critical-practical intent; that is, what we come to understand and accept as true we want finally to promote and act upon as right and good.

Finally, at Level III we turn to the primary religious praxis of confessional naming—coming to our own sense of self-in-collective identity as the progression of tradition. This level is more primarily phenomenal than analytic (Level I) or systematically constructive (Level II). By that I mean that the phenomenon of being grasped by faith and drawn by love has reoriented and transformed us in such a way that at this level we can only *confess* what has happened to us—the root phenomenon of internal history. Theology thus takes on a narrative form—a telling and retelling of who has encountered us and how that new presence brings us not only to the realization and confession of who, what, and how we are in the world but also how we ought to be.[10]

With the interrelationship of the three tri-level schema for properly locating Christian claims for exclusive and singular truth, this Appendix can conclude with only a restatement of what I think we have at least begun as our task. As the title of this Appendix indicates, in many ways we have only been about giving some sense and meaning to the Christian monotheistic claim: "I am the way, the truth, and the life." My intention has been to show how such a claim ought to be used and how it ought not to be used; I have emphasized the care that must be taken when we speak in such terms of full exclusivity and singularity, knowing all the while that at some time and some place such a claim is part of the fundamental Christian monotheistic confession.

NOTES

Introduction

1. See Paul Johnson's *A History of Christianity* (New York: Atheneum Press, 1980) for an excellent one-volume survey of the growth of the Church as a socio-political as well as a religious/theological institution. In fact, Johnson's book is a demonstration of what is required for good historical reconstruction: critical scholarship combined with an acute imagination that breathes life into these ancient periods and makes them relevant.

2. See Rosemary Ruether's *Faith and Fratricide* (New York: Seabury/Crossroad Press, 1979). My interest and general orientation to this issue was influenced by Ruether's "disturbing" book as well as by the efforts of Gregory Baum in Christian-Jewish dialogue.

3. See Ruether, *Faith and Fratricide* and Gregory Baum's "Introduction" to that volume, pp. 1–22. Baum directs us to Alan Davies, *Anti-Semitism and the Christian Mind* (New York: Seabury, 1969); Jules Isaac, *Jesus and Israel* (New York: Holt Rinehart and Winston, 1971); James Parkes, *The Conflict of the Church and the Synagogue* (New York: Atheneum, 1969). See also Charlotte Klein, *Anti-Judaism in Christian Theology*, trans. E. Quinn (Philadelphia: Fortress Press, 1978); *Auschwitz: Beginning of a New Era* (Reflections on the Holocaust), Eva Fleischner, ed. (New York: KTVA, 1977); Lucy Dawidowicz, *The War Against the Jews: 1933–1945* (New York: Bantam, 1976); Alan Davies, ed., *Anti-Semitism and the Foundations of Christianity* (New York: Paulist Press, 1979).

4. See Chiam Potok, *Wandering: The Story of the Jews* (New York: Fawcett-Crest, 1980) for a readable one-volume survey; Robert Gordis, *Judaism in a Christian World* (New York: McGraw-Hill, 1966); F.E. Talmage, ed., *Disputations and Dialogue* (New York: KTVA, 1975); Fleischner, *Auschwitz;* Dawidowicz, *War Against the Jews.* The many works of Elie Wiesel are powerful *re-presentations* of the Jewish struggle for freedom and expression in predominately Christian culture. For ex-

ample, see Elie Wiesel, *A Jew Today* (New York: Random House, 1978). The late Samuel Sandmel's unique perspective of a Jewish scholar with a doctoral degree in the New Testament is expressed with high ecumenical intent in all of his works. For example, see Samuel Sandmel, *We Jews and You Christians* (New York: J.B. Lippincott, 1967). Finally, Rabbi Abraham Heschel and Martin Buber stand as important Jewish contributors to the understanding of Judaism by Christians. For example, see Martin Buber, *Two Types of Faith* (New York: Harper, 1951).

5. See Ruether, *Faith and Fratricide*, pp. 246–251.

6. See Baum, "Introduction," in *Faith and Fratricide*, pp. 11–22.

7. Matthew 16:15–17.

Chapter I

1. By "constructive" orientations to religion and theology I mean efforts at interpretation, reflection, and critical reconstruction that emerge from the milieu of faith, intend to enhance faith, and finally return to faith as a living experience for a final practical check of adequacy.

2. In the Appendix I will deal with the question of how Christian claims can assume the status of exclusive and singular expressions of "truth" and "right." At the same time, I will discuss how such claims of exclusivity and singularity can be abused. This inquiry will necessarily take us to levels of philosophical and theological discussion which are more complex than those of the text. For this reason the issue is addressed in an Appendix for those who wish to probe further.

3. For helpful comments about the interrelationship between thinking and feeling see Robert Johann, "Thought, Feeling, and Reality," in *Building the Human* (New York: Herder and Herder, 1968), pp. 18–20. Johann's essays in this volume function as an excellent summary of the kind of pragmatism that I am suggesting as a normative guide for adequate Christological reconstruction.

4. I will only call attention to the question of the possibility of non-theistic religion that by definition would not use a theology strictly speaking, using instead concepts and phrases oriented by some other (apersonal) transcendental perspective. Such approaches would qualify as religious. They would not qualify, because of their lack of personal and interpersonal metaphors and paradigms, as theistic. Thus, if one were to speak of a transcendental "force" as (in Paul Tillich's term) their "ultimate concern," they would be in a religious not a theistic frame of reference, and certainly not in a Judeo-Christian one. For Tillich's discussion of the notion of religion as "ultimate concern" see his *Systematic Theology* I (Chicago: University of Chicago Press, 1952).

5. For example, I think that the real difficulty of politico/religious

groups such as the "Moral Majority" lies in just this sort of unfortunate mix. Certainly one cannot object to religion or the "churches" speaking out on social and political questions. One can, however, warn against political ideology under the guise of religion, and the implicit denial of critical diversity and plurality.

6. See Ian Ramsey, *Models for Divine Activity* (London: SCM Press, 1973), p. 61. In the same work, and in reference to note 4 above, Ramsey argues that the lack of personal and interpersonal paradigms as models for religious life leads inevitably to an atheistic or at least non-theistic perspective—a "faith" without a God.

Chapter II

1. See, for example the "new Jerusalem passage" in Revelation: "Then I saw a new heaven and a new earth. . . . I saw the holy, city, and the new Jerusalem, coming down from God out of heaven" (Rev 21:1–4 [*JB*]).

2. Joachim Jeremias, *New Testament Theology* (New York: Charles Scribner's Sons, 1971), pp. 122–23.

3. See James M. Robinson, ed., *The Nag Hammadi Library* (New York: Harper & Row, 1977); Elaine Pagels, *The Gnostic Gospels* (New York: Random House, 1979).

4. See Jack T. Sanders, *The New Testament Christological Hymns* (Cambridge: The University Press, 1971), pp. 24–25.

5. *Ibid.*, pp. 24–25.

6. Martin Hengel, *The Son of God: The Origin of Christology and the History of Jewish-Hellenistic Religion* (Philadelphia: Fortress Press, 1976), p. 43.

7. *Ibid.*, p. 56.

8. *Ibid.*, p. 46.

9. *Ibid.*, p. 47.

10. *Ibid.*, pp. 48–49.

11. *Ibid.*, p. 50.

12. See Philo, *Quaest. Gen.* 4.97 and quoted in Hengel, *The Son of God*, p. 50.

13. Hengel, *The Son of God*, pp. 52–53.

14. *Ibid.*, pp. 51–56.

15. *Ibid.*, pp. 59–60.

16. *Ibid.*, pp. 86, 85–88.

17. *Ibid.*, pp. 86–87.

18. *Ibid.*, pp. 77–83.

19. *Ibid.*, p. 73.

20. See Jn 1:1–16.

21. See Hengel, *The Son of God,* pp. 59–66.

22. *Ibid.,* p. 88.

23. Gabriel Marcel's notion of the difference between a *mystery* and a *problem* has important implications for our discussion. See "On the Ontological Mystery," in Gabriel Marcel, *The Philosophy of Existentialism* (Secaucus, N.J.: Citadel Press, 1956), pp. 9–46. Basically, Marcel notes how mysteries surround and envelop us—drawing us in, so to speak. Problems, on the other hand, seem to stand apart from us waiting to be observed extrinsically, ordered, controlled and solved.

Chapter III

1. See David Tracy's notion of the phenomena of faith and religion as the product of particular and unique "limit experiences" as well as his designation of religious discourse as "limit language" in Tracy, *Blessed Rage for Order* (New York: Seabury, 1975).

2. See Gordon Kaufman, "Theology as Construction," in *An Essay on Theological Method* (Chico, California: Scholars Press, 1975), pp. 19–40. See also David Tracy, *The Analogical Imagination* (New York: Crossroad, 1981). Even though both Kaufman and Tracy utilize the category of "imagination" as foundational for theological construction, there are basic differences in their work. Kaufman's emphasis is on the process of constructing theological concepts and ideas. In this regard see also Gordon Kaufman, *The Theological Imagination: Constructing the Concept of God* (Philadelphia: Westminster, 1981). Tracy, on the other hand, emphasizes the radical interconnection between the "event" of faith and critical theological construction as an integrated public life experience. See, for example, Tracy, *The Analogical Imagination,* pp. 329–32, and Chapter Ten, "A Christian Systematic Analogical Imagination," pp. 405–455. Tracy more than Kaufman comes closer to what I mean by "constructive theology." Of importance as well is H. Richard Niebuhr's earlier discussion of "Imagination and Reason" in H.R. Niebuhr, *The Meaning of Revelation* (New York: Macmillan, 1941), pp. 67–80.

3. Paul Johnson, *A History of Christianity,* p. 89.

4. See Van Harvey, *A Handbook of Theological Terms* (New York: Macmillan, 1964), *passim.* Harvey's book is a helpful tool for identifying and ordering the various claims for orthodox doctrine in this period, and a valuable study-book in general.

5. *Ibid.,* pp. 28; 27–29.

6. *Ibid.,* pp. 27–29.

7. *Ibid.,* p. 28.

8. Along with Harvey, see Paul Johnson's discussion of this period in *A History of Christianity,* pp. 87–96.

9. Van Harvey, *A Handbook of Theological Terms*, pp. 27–29.
10. Richard A. Norris, ed. and trans., *The Christological Controversy* (Philadelphia: Fortress Press, 1980), p. 159.
11. *Ibid.*
12. Van Harvey, *A Handbook of Theological Terms*, p. 123.
13. *Ibid.*, p. 50.
14. *Ibid.*, p. 171.
15. *Ibid.*, p. 154.
16. My understanding of a critical-practical approach to interpreting scriptural texts as well as doctrines and dogmas (here and throughout) has been greatly influenced by the hermeneutic theory of Hans-Georg Gadamer developed in his book *Truth and Method* (New York: Seabury Press, 1975). (First published in German in 1960.)
17. Hans Küng, *On Being a Christian*, trans. by Edward Quinn (New York: Pocket Books, 1978, pp. 122–26. (First published in German in 1974.)
18. For a more complete discussion of these trends see Gerald O'Collins, *What Are They Saying About Jesus?* (New York: Paulist Press, 1977).
19. *Ibid.*
20. See Gibson Winter, "Human Science and Ethics in a Creative Society," *Cultural Hermeneutics* 1 (1973), 145–76.
21. See Rosemary Reuther, *Faith and Fratricide.*
22. Paul Tillich, *The New Being* (New York: Scribner's, 1955), p. 18.

Chapter IV

1. See Gustavo Gutiérrez, *A Theology of Liberation*, trans. G. Inda and J. Eagleston (Maryknoll, N.Y.: Orbis, 1973), for a discussion of "orthopraxis."
2. See Ian Ramsey, *Models for Divine Activity* (London: SCM Press, 1973), pp. 57–61.
3. See H. Richard Niebuhr's discussion of "radical monotheism" in "The Idea of Radical Monotheism" in H. Richard Niebuhr, *Radical Monotheism and Western Culture* (New York: Harper Torchbooks, 1970), pp. 24–37.
4. We will never advance our understanding of an adequate Christian doctrine of the Trinity by thinking in primarily numerical or arithmetic terms. Notions of "one in three" or "three in one" have been and will always remain logical contradictions, not mysteries. Despite common homiletic appeals, theology cannot retreat from the challenge of Trinitarian explanation.
5. While I am certain that Christians will never cease talking of God as "Father" (nor should they) to indicate God as source and con-

cerned parent, we are beginning to see that the metaphor of "Mother" can be just as fruitful. Certainly the advances of modern science over the last centuries indicate that both father and mother equally share in reproduction and generation of new life. Parental care and concern is equally shared by both father and mother. *New* Christian and, indeed, theistic speech can easily and correctly use these two meaningful metaphors. And further, such a dual utilization has moral importance in the creation of a more responsible Church—a Church more responsive to the legitimate complaints of women who have historically suffered the oppression of male ecclesiastical domination. Basic and "root" metaphors indicate meanings and have socio-political effects. In a rather twisted theological and moral logic, a "male" God historically indicated (and for some now indicates) a male-dominant Church.

6. Related to the above note, we will certainly continue to speak of the historical *Jesus* in male terms. However, the meaning of the resurrected *Christ* finally transcends sexual discriminations.

7. The Greek term *anamnesis* is often used to indicate the particular type of Christian remembrance of Jesus in our liturgical celebration—an active remembering that brings presence in intense encounters of faith. This notion of making present in memory is not unusual in the world religions. In Judaism the presence of God's great deeds of liberation and covenant are recalled and, in that, renewed in the Passover meal. Because such presence is experienced through memorial celebration does not make it any less real.

8. "Modalism is an interpretation of the doctrine of the Trinity in which the PERSONS of the Trinity are viewed as modes of divine action rather than as eternal and essential distinctions within the divine nature itself": (Van Harvey, *A Handbook of Theological Terms*, p. 152).

9. See Hans Küng, *On Being a Christian*, pp. 122–26.

10. See Edward Schillebeeckx, *Interim Report of the Books Jesus and Christ* (New York: Crossroad, 1981), pp. 74–93. (For his comprehensive Christology, see Schillebeeckx's books *Jesus* and *Christ*).

11. See H. R. Niebuhr, "The Idea of Radical Monotheism."

12. *Ibid.*

13. See H. R. Niebuhr, "The Idea of Radical Monotheism," and H. R. Niebuhr *Christ and Culture* (New York: Harper, 1951).

14. The verbal connotations of "being" (esse) indicate the dynamic state of action, development, and process that seem to be our human experience of continually coming to be in the world. Our process of coming to be is intrinsically intersubjective and social as we respond to the call and action of others upon us. Whatever union we might attain with others (as well as the sense of self that emerges from such unions) is directly dependent on the intensity and intimacy of these responsive interperson-

al engagements. Thus, when we look for *apt metaphors* for theologically *imagining* the union between God and Jesus, we will find them around and within our own human experience of being with others.

15. See, for example, the Book of Hosea, The Song of Solomon, and Paul's metaphor of the intimate union between wife and husband as a model for the interrelationship of Christ and the Church.

16. It is important to remember that the New Testament cosmological imagery is thoroughly bound up with the science of its ancient worldview. We can no more be called upon to canonize such images than be asked to accept en masse the ancient sciences. This is not to say that the ancient cosmological symbols and myths have no value, or that they cannot be critically utilized within certain bounds. Nature imagery is still a vital resource for posing the power and, indeed, majesty of the divine-human encounter. (See Ian Ramsey's excellent discussion of nature imagery for God in *Models for Divine Activity*, pp. 1–14). However, it is to say that whatever the ancient *and* modern sciences have to teach us, whatever resource they might offer for models and metaphors of interrelating God and world (God and Jesus), we know that they will be variable and changeable, as will our efforts to make critical and practical use of them for our God-language.

17. See Nikos Kazantzakis' series of meditations on this theme in his *The Saviors of God* (New York: Simon & Schuster, 1960).

18. The question of Jesus' personal sinlessness may be as inappropriate to probe as that question for any other person. But rather than totally avoid it, can we not say that particular temptations or sins in the life of Jesus (as in our own lives) do not in themselves constitute ultimate infidelity? The prospect for conversion, rededication, and change remains constant. Regardless of the particulars of Jesus' personal moral history (about which we know very little) we confess that he was *finally faithful* in a way that is normative and paradigmatic for Christians.

19. For my own attempts to further probe the implications of the paradigm of dialogue for socio-political as well as religious life, see Joseph Monti, *Ethics and Public Policy: The Conditions of Public Moral Discourse* (Washington, D.C.: The University Press of America, 1982).

20. This phrase, "our word for God," is used intentionally to indicate that speaking the name "Jesus Christ" has a twofold meaning for Christians—*our word spoken to God* and *our word for God's most intense involvement in the world,* God's dialogic union with Jesus, the Christ.

Appendix

1. See David Tracy's discussion of "The Meaning, Meaningfulness, and Truth of God-Language," in *Blessed Rage for Order,* pp. 172–203.

2. See Paul Tillich's discussion of the "grasp" of faith and the "draw" of love in his *Systematic Theology* III (Chicago: University of Chicago Press, 1963). See especially Chapter Two: "The Spiritual Presence," pp. 129–138, and Chapter Three: "The Divine Spirit and the Ambiguities of Life," pp. 217–245.

3. See again Ian Ramsey's important discussion of the necessity of personal and interpersonal metaphors and images for theistic faith in *Models for Divine Activity*, pp. 57–61 and *passim*.

4. There is an obvious circularity here but it is not of the "vicious" variety. At this level of phenomenological identification—levels of deep interpretation of who, what and how we are in the world—"normal" rules of logical procedure often do not apply.

5. The maximalist monotheistic claim is "I am the Lord your God, there is no other." The maximalist Christian claim is indicated in the title of this Appendix: "I am the way, the truth, and the life" (John 14:6). It is perhaps understandable that the more "conservative" Christian denominations highlight this text and its claim for exclusive and singular truth, while the more "liberal" denominations either avoid or dilute it. It is my argument, however, that neither the conservative abuse nor the liberal lack of use is adequate. A faithful confession of Christian monotheism demands that we adopt this and similar claims; a critical theology requires that we understand how such passages can and cannot be legitimately used.

6. See H. Richard Niebuhr, *The Meaning of Revelation* (New York: Macmillan, 1941), pp. 44–54 and Chapter II in general, "The Story of Our Life," pp. 32–66.

7. *Ibid.*, 44.

8. *Ibid.*, 45.

9. See Chapter I, n. 1.

10. If we want more specifically to locate forms of religious and theological language we can note, for example, that much of New Testament language emerges at Level III with some mergence to Level II. Much of the theology done in ecclesial contexts is—or ought to be—engaged at Level II. Other forms of the praxis of theological language in the Church (homilies, liturgical prayers and creeds, pastoral guidance, etc.) are to a greater or lesser degree found in the mergence of Levels II and III. Descriptions and analyses of theological ideas and systems and the effects of religious and theological claims are engaged at Level I with some shading at times to Level II.

DATE DUE

APR 18 '96			
DEC 31 '99			